Successful PARENT, SUCCESSFUL CHILD

10 Things Every Single Parent Needs to Know

ALEXANDRA BRAUNI

SUCCESSFUL PARENT, SUCCESSFUL CHILD

10 Things Every Single Parent Needs to Know

ALEXANDRA BRAUNI

Published by Concepcion Munoz-Garcia

First Edition

Printed in the United States of America

ISBN: 978-0-578-23740-4

www.alexandraBrauni.com

www.successfulparentsuccessfulchild.com

Disclaimer

It should be noted that, although the examples are based on real stories, most of the names and are fictitious, in order to protect the identity of the protagonists.

The information contained in this book is for general information. No amount of information can guarantee success or profitability. The information must be used in a judicious manner to be effective. The publisher and the author accept no responsibility for any individual's or organization's business outcomes as a result of following the advice in this book. Readers are encouraged to use common sense and discretion while using any information in this book.

Table Of Contents

Acknowledgments

SPECIAL THANKS GO TO:

My son, Alexander, who helped me to evolve and inspired me to write this book.

My family, who led me to success without pretending.

My friend Maria Díez de Gispert, who waited for me and showed me unconditional friendship, her husband Xavier Bombí, and their wonderful kids, Guillem, Xavi, and Jaume.

My friends and Alexander's godparents, Estela Franco and Lucas Domínguez.

My friend Per Wimmer because he was a source of inspiration for me and reminded me that life must always be lived with passion.

My lifelong friend, Eva Badia, for still being there.

My friend Clara Troncoso and her great family who supported me when I arrived in New York City.

Andrea Vanryken, my editor, for her great work and dedication in bringing this book to light.

Writers and coaches Raia King and Cristina Smith for their support and helpful suggestions on how to make my book better.

Dedication

This book is dedicated, in a very special way to my son Alexander and to all single parents and their offspring, no matter what gender they belong to. However, I would like to extend this dedication to all the dreamers who never gave up and to all those people who are still in search of that lighthouse that will make their dream a reality. Start walking because, on the other side of the river, there are many of us waiting for you.

Alexandra Brauni

Introduction

A few weeks ago, I had a conversation with a friend, a single father, during which he confessed to me that it's been very difficult for him to combine single parenting and what he really wants to do in his life. He literally told me, "My life sucks, and I can't change it. My family, my son...everything conditions me. I'm trapped. I can't escape, and I survive the way I can. That's all." Those hopeless, heartbreaking words made me think. I knew many people who have expressed a similar feeling, and curiously, most of them are single parents. I thought it was time to share my story and thus offer a different approach to what I consider "living" or "vegetating" as a human being, especially when we are single parents, with the limitations that this entails.

Since childhood, I have been a very curious, very active, and untraditional person. I am the oldest of three children and the only woman. I was brought up in a family of traders who ran three bakeries in a village near Barcelona, and the only thing I heard from my father, day after day, was "Money is the most important thing in life. A penny in your pocket is your best friend." My brothers were always more obedient, but I, as I was and am a rebel by nature, decided at the age of eleven to go against my father, dedicate myself to writing and publishing poetry, and become a fervent reader. I still remember my first interview for a local newspaper in which they published my poems and cataloged me as a child prodigy. A girl who had been brought up to be "a wife, a mother, and little else," a girl who had her dreams and her future stolen from her but who fought to the end to get them back, and in the end, succeeded. I decided to go through life with little baggage, to study, to go to college—despite my family's opposition—and to change my circumstances, my life.

I remember one day while walking through the streets of my city, something struck me and left me absorbed. Some words painted on the front of a house would mark my life and encourage me to move forward without ever looking back. I spent a long time reading those phrases and thinking about what their meaning might be. Then a neighbor told me that the house was an inheritance with the condition that no one, under any pretext, would erase those words. I was fascinated by both the history and the meaning of those verses written in Catalan: "Caminant de per aquí, no perdis de la memòria, que la vida es el camí que porta a l'eterna glòria si bé la uses fins al fi." Translated into English, they mean: "Walking this way, don't lose your memory, that life is the road that leads to eternal glory if you use it to the end."

A lot has happened in my life since then. I have traveled the world, lived for seven years in London, and now reside in the United States. And although that may all sound like a road of roses, it has also been a journey filled with thorns, especially after becoming a single mother. So, I can understand the feelings of frustration and helplessness that plague single parents. That is why, using my experience, I am going to give you ten guidelines that all single parents need to know if they want to succeed. These recommendations have helped me, after arriving alone with my eight-year-old son in a city as competitive as New York, to achieve a good position and live the American dream.

This book is structured into ten chapters, each one dedicated to a guideline. Every chapter documents life experiences from me and others. Experiences rich in knowledge, with which I have vibrated. I have grown as a human being, and they have made me value what is important in our existence: the simple, everyday things, and the moments…always the moments.

This book will bring you hope. It will prove to you that if I was able to change my life despite my family environment, despite my circumstances as a single mother, and succeed, you can too. I have always been very discreet about my private life, but I think it is time to share part of it with you and show you, through my experiences, that you can be a single and successful parent at the same time. Give me your hand and accompany me through this fantastic journey.

Chapter 1

LISTEN TO YOUR INNER VOICE

Listen to and Follow Your Inner Voice Before Making an Important Decision in Your Life.

"Life is an exciting journey, rich with feelings and experiences. Walk into your dream and enjoy it. If I can do it, you can do it."
—*Alexandra Brauni*

B efore embarking on the path that will take you where you want to go as a human being and as a parent, you need to have clear ideas. To achieve this, I advise you to take your time to think, listen to your heart, and discover your most intimate desires. Do not let yourself be guided by other people's opinions. You are going to be the captain of this ship, and even if the crew has different opinions, remember that the captain always has the last word. Listening and asking for opinions at this time is of little use. Each person will give you a different one, depending on their experiences and fears, which will only confuse you and delay the journey you are about to take. Your child should never be a hindrance. On the contrary, consider him/her a companion on this road. Though it may be hard at times to combine caring for your child with striving to achieve your goal, there are ways to do it. I did it, and so can you. And as the years pass, when you look back, you'll realize how worthwhile it has been sharing these life experiences with your child. Remember: Children are great imitators.

From a very young age, I had to deal with situations in which I was forced to make big decisions. And in those moments, as difficult as they were, I took my time, thought carefully about my options, and listened to my deepest feelings. I would make a determination without turning back, omitting other people's opinions. When I was eighteen years old, I started a relationship with a boy who was very well-positioned and whose family was friends of my parents. As our relationship progressed, he became more and more enthusiastic, until one day he proposed to me the old-fashioned way, ring in hand. At that time both families were delighted, but despite my short experience, something told me that I could not accept that proposal of love. I still remember when my father knocked on the door of my room one night and told me that I should consider leaving my university career and start a family with my fiancé, who was an excellent person with money, and that after our wedding I would no longer need to work, and therefore finishing my university career, according to him, was meaningless. I was up all night thinking. The easy would be to accept the marriage proposal, live a comfortable life, and give up my dreams. I was confused. On the one hand, I wanted to satisfy my family, but on the other, there was me and my desire to live, to know the world. In the end, after much reflection,

I decided to listen to myself, to my inner voice. I asked myself what I really wanted. Many fears, doubts, and mixed emotions emerged. Finally, the next day, I confronted my father and told him that I had already made an irrevocable decision, that I was going to leave my boyfriend and finish my career. It should be noted that this break up brought about grim consequences for my family. To begin with, my mother packed my bag and put it on my doorstep with these words: "You've lost your mind. You're never going to find a man like that. I wish I had had a chance like that when I was young." However, my decision had been made, and there was no turning back. I had been honest with myself, had not betrayed myself, and had chosen with my heart. Today, I know I picked the right path, but at that time it was a really difficult choice.

In the example above, I was single, with no plans to have children, and the decisions I made only affected me. When you have kids you have to think twice because they're involved too, but you still have to make choices while being honest with yourself and with your feelings.

Alexandra Brauni

After breaking off my engagement, I moved to Barcelona and started to combine my two professions, teaching and journalism, to make a living. At that stage of my life, I was so immersed in my work, travels, and parties that I forgot the idea of marriage, and of course, children. Forming a family for me, for many years, was synonymous with "chains" and lack of freedom. My family had been so preoccupied with the traditional role that women should play in society that all I wanted was to focus on my profession and enjoy it. And so my life went, until fate, capriciously, took me, a group of friends, and my brother to a Caribbean country par excellence: Cuba. There I met the man who would later become my husband and father of my only child.

When my son was born, my priorities changed, even more so when I was in England and separated and left alone to take care of my little one. From then on, what no one had ever gotten me to do before, my son did. I changed my habits, became more responsible, and when I had to make a decision, I always thought about my little one. However, though being a single mother limited me in many activities, I never, I repeat, *never* gave up on dreaming and moving forward, overcoming the obstacles that I encountered along the way. I turned a "No" or "Maybe" into a resounding "*yes*" through my work and my perseverance, dedication, and strategy. I will talk about these four elements for success in future chapters.

There are parents who, when they are alone with their children, leave them in the care of grandparents or other relatives in order to move around more freely. I believe that children need to walk hand in hand with their parents, learn from their mistakes, and celebrate their successes. This is an experience of life and love that will leave an everlasting mark on our children.

In 2008, my husband, my son, and I left Barcelona and settled in London, England. Like all principles, ours were hard and seemed even more so in a foreign country. I remember that when we arrived, we shared a house with a Colombian family who had a daughter, and, after my marital separation in 2009, the lady of the house asked me why I wouldn't consider giving my son up for adoption, since she and her husband had fallen in love with my little boy. First, I took it as a joke. Then I realized she was serious. I spent a long time talking to her about this because I couldn't understand why a mother would give her child up for adoption for any reason. At that time I was alone with little money, and someone else might have agreed because being a single parent with a baby is really complicated. But I was clear about it: My son would always accompany me wherever I went, under any and all circumstances, and that's how it has been until now. It was also clear to me that I would fight to the end to achieve my dream and that my son would come with me and witness my efforts and achievements.

I know people who complain all the time about not having dedicated themselves to their desired profession or not having realized that dream they've always had since childhood, and they always end up looking for excuses—either because of their children or because of lack of money, time, etc. I currently live in Brooklyn, and I recently had a conversation with Juan, a neighbor of a certain age who lives in my neighborhood and whom I sometimes pass on the street. One day, while we were talking, Juan confessed to me that he felt frustrated because despite being an American and having had many opportunities to prosper, he had not been able to meet his expectations nor fulfill his dream of becoming a lawyer due to family obligations. However, he added that he was happy for his son since his wife was a lawyer. I did not quite understand what his desire to be a lawyer had to do with his daughter-in-law having this profession. That old man seemed to me a clear example of the frustration we can feel at the end of our days if we do not realize our dream in life because of "what I could have been but never was." I also thought that Juan was self-deceived, believing that he was sacrificing his life "to be a good father," when in reality he had let himself be paralyzed by the fear of leaving his comfort zone. He lacked the courage to take the reins of his life and fight for his happiness. The fact is that the words "sacrifice" and "self-deception" are often handled by our subconscious the wrong way and get confused. The truth is that in life you have to be brave and make decisions. It may be that at a certain moment you cannot run in the direction you most want to take, but if you can postpone the urge for a short period of time, you can then take control of your life and do what really satisfies you.

Here's one powerful example: Years ago I was in a very complicated situation in which I had to make a very delicate decision. In 2007, I entered the American Green Card draw, and in 2008, when I arrived in London, I was told that I had won it. I was overjoyed. I had visited New York years before with a friend and had felt at home. I really identified with the city and the American people. After that experience, and after winning the Green Card, it was clear to me that this was a golden opportunity I needed to take advantage of. But a year later my marriage separation came about, and I only had two options: either to go to the United States at that time and leave my son with his father, or wait until after the divorce so my son could come with me. The

United Kingdom is a great country for which I have nothing but praise—except for its always gray and rainy climate, which can seem almost unbearable. However, as a journalist, teacher, and enterprising woman, I saw clearly that all my dreams could come true in America, so I refused to give up that opportunity. The question was: What would I do with my son in that situation? I knew that, as a single mother, taking the road to the United States was going to be hard, but leaving my son would be much harder. So, I did what I advised at the beginning of this chapter: I reflected, thought carefully about my decision, and then listened to my inner voice. It told me to leave but to be patient—to wait for the right moment for my son to come with me. And so I did. I didn't let myself be influenced by other people's opinions, such as that of the Colombian lady who insisted on adopting my son, or the lawyers who advised me to stay in London so that everything would be easier, that New York would always be there for me to visit. But nothing and nobody could convince me. My inner voice was strong and clear. So, my decision was already made. I would leave with my child and fight until the end to achieve my dream.

Seven years of hard battles in court followed, during which I grew really exhausted and sometimes lost my motivation, but I never forgot my goal, my dream, for which I fought fiercely until I was finally successful. I always knew what I wanted and that I was going to achieve it; it was just a matter of time and persistence. As a good friend of mine would say: "In life, the most important thing is not to lose yourself and to have hope. The rest, there is a solution." Well, during those seven very hard years of waiting, I always kept the flame of hope burning and was always aware that the situation was temporary and that everything would be solved—and it was. It took seven years of court visits to legally enable my son to come with me to the United States. At first, I hired lawyers, but they were so expensive that I ended up going to court alone and representing myself in front of the judge.

It was in 2015 when my extension to enter the United States was about to end that I had to make one of the most painful decisions of my life. It was my last trial. If I didn't win, I would have to give up my Green Card, my dreams, my future, and stay in England for good. So, I took a chance. I don't know where I got the courage to say the words, but I told the judge that I was giving custody of my son to my ex-husband, who was present in the courtroom. A deathly silence came over the courtroom, and the judge, astonished, asked me, "So, are you leaving?" to which I nodded affirmative and gave the dry and emphatic answer, "Yes." Fortunately, as the judge was about to give custody to my ex-husband, my ex requested a private meeting with me, and we were finally able to work things out amicably. So, thanks to my patience and determination, I was finally able to take my son to the United States, and we have been able to live this dream together. Today I look back and know that I have learned from that hard experience, I learned a lot. I became a better person. I tested my stamina and came to understand that "power is possible," that "love can overcome all obstacles," and that any sacrifice made is worthwhile. Today, when life smiles at me, I know that what I have lived through with my child is an incredible life experience that will unite us forever.

Alexandra Brauni

I wonder what would have become of my son's life and mine if I had not persevered, if I had not had a clear direction to guide me, if I had decided to throw in the towel and surrender to other people's opinions about what I should or should not do. Fortunately, I listened to my inner voice and let it guide me to the right path. You may be in a similar situation while reading this book, or you may be in a conflicting situation that has put you between a rock and a hard place. My advice is to take a chance. Happiness is priceless, and you must strive for it without hesitation. People are molded by the choices they make. We are constantly choosing what we want and what we don't, from the clothes we wear in the morning before we leave the house to how we want our coffee when we go to the coffee shop on the corner. These are all small decisions that shape our reality and our world. I know from my own experience that making rash decisions when children are involved may not be best. I advise you to take your time and always *"Listen to your inner voice before making an important decision in your life."*

In the next chapter, I will show you some techniques I used in some of my worst moments. After settling first in London and then, seven years later, in New York, completely isolated from my family and lifelong friends, I experienced a deep sense of loneliness. At that time, my son became my only comfort and the engine that drove me on. I had to give up all the comforts I enjoyed in Barcelona, my hometown, and learn to reinvent myself.

Chapter 2

KEEP A DIARY, FOLLOW A STRATEGY, AND ENJOY AT THE SAME TIME

Keep a Diary to Write Down Your Dream, Your Strategy to Achieve That Dream, the Time You Put into It, And Your Disappointments. Learn How to Distract Yourself During Your Low Moments.

Everyone finds distractions in different places. Some people go shopping, others stay with friends for a few drinks and to talk, while still others—like me—paint their house. When we lived in London, and after spending a year in a hostel, we moved to a two-room flat near the city. I was feeling a bit stressed out at the time with all the changes in my life, so I started painting my apartment and eventually finished the entire flat. This may sound absurd, but that activity was my therapy. It relaxed me a lot and saved me the expense of hiring a painter. Another of my favorite hobbies when depressed is reading or watching autobiographies on TV. I have always been interested in the lives of ordinary people who have outdone themselves, who have something to say. So, I would distract myself with movies or books based on real stories, inspired by people who have been in critical situations, and who, thanks to their determination and perseverance, finally achieved their goal. These people dared to break social norms and be authentic, and for me, during this period of instability in my life, they were a great source of inspiration. Some folk I learned about were single parents, and others were not, but they were always characterized by the same values: courage, strength, and persistence in the face of adversity.

If you are currently going through a separation, a complicated divorce in which you are solely in charge of your children and have little family support, or if your situation is different but you still feel demoralized, I advise you to watch these types of films. If you like to read, you can also find such inspiring stories in book-form. Most of these people come from difficult circumstances, and after overcoming them succeeded in what they set out to do, despite all the obstacles encountered along the way. You will relate to many of these people and be taught how and encouraged to go on. Afterward—and I assume that you already have a diary—I advise you to open it and spend a few minutes writing down what has impressed you about the film or book and then consider how you can put the strategies described into practice to start you on the road to your personal and professional success. Of course, first, you have to be clear about where you want to go and what your goal is—which I talked about in the first chapter. Writing your goals and strategies down will help you to convince your subconscious that you have already started down the road to success, and so you will walk with more confidence and poise because your subconscious will have already received the message. The words we write and read often take on a strength and life of their own. They become reality. Think about that, and if you don't have a journal yet, get one. This will be your bedside book, the recipient of your dreams and achievements, written in your own handwriting. On paper, you can list the strategy or strategies you plan to follow to achieve your final goal and the approximate time you will need to achieve them. I advise you to set small goals for yourself at first, which will make the road to success easier for you as you achieve them.

It is possible that, at this time, you have other more important concerns that occupy your mind, and you may consider it absurd to spend your time watching movies, reading self-help books, and writing your impressions down in a journal. But believe me, this strategy is much more useful and effective than you might think. I've tried it on several occasions during which my only companion in the struggle was my son, where I had lost absolutely everything and was far from my country, my people, my comfort zone. I was totally isolated. And it was in those moments of desperation that this material, which I will now tell you about, was of great support to me. By the way, and speaking of your child, don't ever feel like he or she in the way. It is true that a child can be an obstacle that can make it more difficult for a single parent to advance quickly toward his/her goal—particularly when that child is a baby—but it is also a motor that drives you to overcome the difficulties you find along the way, so put aside your impatience and think positively.

Each film I'm going to recommend has also been published in book-form, so you can decide which format you prefer.

1. *The Pursuit of Happyness*: This film is based on the life of Chris Gardner in San Francisco in the '70s. Chris, a middle-aged black man abandoned by his wife lives in extreme poverty with his young son while working as a salesman and studying to achieve his dream of becoming a stockbroker. I've seen this movie around fifty times, and I'm still discovering new details that inspire me regarding this single, homeless father, who is currently a billionaire. This

story helped me get through my lowest moments in the UK when I had no contact with my family and friends and was completely broke, living alone with my son in a homeless hostel in Clapton, a district of East London, England, in the London Borough of Hackney. This happened in 2009, shortly after my marital separation and after leaving my shared home with the Colombian family. I could only work part-time since I was on my own and looking after my son. The rent in London was quite high, so there was no alternative but to turn to charity—it was either that or end up sleeping on the streets, which would have been devastating for a toddler just over two years old. So, I accepted the help of the British government without hesitation, and we moved into a hostel for the homeless. We lived in a studio with a bathroom and kitchen, which led to another studio inhabited by a woman with alcoholism. Upstairs lived a boy in his twenties who had AIDS and with whom I became friendly.

We had been in that hostel in North London for a few months, the second hostel for me and my son, and although it was more welcoming than the first, my financial and emotional situation was very unstable. It had been a little over a year since I had left my country, completely ruined because of some risky investments I had made that went so bad I lost everything I had materially. As a result, major disagreements arose with my family that completely destabilized me. When I left Barcelona, I had been well situated, as I was working as a teacher and as director of a small local television station. However, due to a lot of external pressure, I decided to leave all that behind, change my ways, and move to the UK for a while. Imagine for a moment that you are born in a golden cradle where you never have any economic shortage, and then due to life circumstances, you lose everything—and on top of that your relationship breaks down and you are left alone with a baby in a foreign country whose language you have not mastered. What would you do?

Shortly after we moved into the hostel, my son got sick with swine flu and had a high fever for more than a week. We managed to bring it down with medication, but soon after it came back up again. I repeatedly called the paramedics, who advised me to keep him at home. My son got worse and worse, and I could hardly work because someone had to take care of him. The situation became so critical that my little boy almost died. If it wasn't for my insistence in taking him to a crowded hospital, where he wasn't properly diagnosed, I wouldn't be writing this book right now. My son was finally diagnosed with the onset of pneumonia caused by swine flu, and after being prescribed the appropriate medication, he was cured. It was like being immersed in the worst nightmare, completely alone, without any help and in a country completely foreign to me. As you can imagine, the experience was very hard, but as I have always done, I fought to the end and was able to overcome that traumatic situation. Although it seems absurd, in those moments of supreme loneliness, of silences without response, I found my biggest inspiration in the movies I watched, the books I read, and in writing my diary, since I was locked up for many hours. I lived in constant chaos; in those moments I could not even glimpse the end of the tunnel. It was then that I happened to see *The Pursuit of Happyness* on television, and that movie opened my eyes to another reality. It served as my motivation to keep going. I was impressed by the strength of Chris, a single father, to move forward and overcome all his obstacles. What I liked most was how under no circumstances did he allow himself to be separated from his son. It's an exemplary story and really motivating film because it extols the role of the "single father," so little valued in our society against that of "single mother," and it is a clear example of the great work that men can do with their children in a similar situation. Many people believe that the role of a single parent can only be properly performed by a woman. This is not so. Chris Gardner is a clear example of this.

However, I also enjoyed some nice and rewarding experiences from that period of uncertainty when my son and I were living at Clapton Inn. I remember vividly when Estela and her now-husband, Lucas, agreed to be my son's godparents. They traveled to London to attend my son's baptism. Alexander was almost three years old at the time and extremely restless. He used to escape from the church all the time, and Lucas spent the whole religious celebration behind him, running in and out of the church. I remember that experience in a loving and grateful way. Estela, a great lawyer, and Lucas, a retired businessman and painter par excellence, belonged to my circle of friends in Barcelona. They were some of only a few folk in my life who knew about my situation and showed me unconditional appreciation and support. It is in those moments that you realize who loves you for who you are and when true friendship is forged. I only have words of praise for Alexander's godparents.

Despite the work limitations I encountered as a single mother, I decided to look for a way out of that hostel and find a better place to live. So, I entered a public housing lottery. After a year in that homeless shelter, I was selected in the lottery and offered a very well-located, two-room apartment near Waterloo Station and the city. The rent I paid was really cheap, about £400 a month, so from then on, my financial situation started to improve. I continued to give private Spanish lessons in order to survive, and as my English improved, I was able to validate my teaching qualifications in the UK and start working as a substitute teacher in some schools in London. Another difficult task on my agenda at the time was to find a reliable caregiver for my son, who was just over three years old, barely speaking, and quite naughty. I'll tell you more about that in another chapter. Right now, I'd like to recommend a few more films that may help you in your low moments, as they did with me.

2. The second film that I recommend, although some people may be too sensitive to watch the entire film due to its unflinching realism is *Homeless to Harvard*. It is based on the life of Liz Murray, from the Bronx, who lived through the hell of having both of her parents ravaged by drugs and AIDS, barely went to school, and who after the death of her mother, worked hard and managed to get to the prestigious Harvard University. I discovered this film in New York in 2015, also during a difficult period of my life. I had just arrived with my son at a friend's house in South Brooklyn, with only $2,000

in my pocket because of the cost of the long legal process I had endured in the UK, and working a part-time job at a Catholic school in Brooklyn. For me, it was a relief to arrive back in a foreign country and have a friend, someone to trust and support me. My friend had a child two years younger than mine and was pregnant again. My son and I slept on an air mattress on the floor in her son's room. The first few days, my friend stayed with my son while I worked, then I found a school for him near her house. However, fifteen days after we moved into her house, because of our disagreements and lack of space, we had to start looking for another house to relocate to as soon as possible. For the time being, we had to share the house again, this time with strangers, but it was either that or go back to London, where I still had my apartment. I know that another person in my situation, alone with an eight-year-old child, would have considered going back to England, but I am one of those who think that you should never look back, only forward. So, I decided to take a risk, even though I was starting from scratch and my new beginning was really uncertain. Once again I was alone with my son but, as always, ready to fight to the end to make a place for myself in that competitive city of skyscrapers.

I remember going around looking for a room to stay in, but after telling each landlord I had a little boy, they would say the room was taken, and so on and so forth. It was a desperate time. I would come home from work, spend the day looking at ads, and then calling anything with potential, to no avail. I would say the word "child," and all the doors would close. But as fate would have it, on a lamppost in front of the Catholic school where I worked, someone put up an ad looking for a roommate. I called and went to see the room; it was small and overlooked the kitchen. There I talked to a Mexican woman in her upper 20s, and she introduced me to her two children and husband. Luckily, the woman and I had good chemistry, and she rented the room to me. Even though the bedroom was small, and the kitchen countertop—always full of dishes to be washed—was infested with cockroaches, I felt like the luckiest woman in the world to have found a corner where we could stay. So, you see, it was hard to settle in with my son in New York at first. I know that it would have been much easier to do it alone, but these are the kinds of unique experiences, full of struggle, survival, despair, and hope, that unite people and make them stronger and more authentic. My son has seen me fight with life and grow discouraged but still get up again the next day and go on, never giving up, and that has been a great learning experience for him. It was during this period, while I was looking for a place to stay, that I had the opportunity to see *Homeless to Harvard* for the first time. It's an inspiring story that encouraged me to keep going. I said to myself, "If she can, sleeping on the street, with drug-addicted parents, without going to school, so can I." I told myself that I had already achieved an important part of my dream—moving to New York—and I knew in advance that it wasn't going to be easy. But I had dreamed for seven years of stepping onto the asphalt of this city and imbuing myself with its energy and vitality. So, at that moment, I could only be grateful to be there, accompanied by my son. Even though we had little money at that time, I was determined that I would resist, just as Liz Murray in *Homeless to Harvard* did. After all, my dream had just begun, and most importantly, I was determined to share it with my son. So, I encouraged myself by recalling several complex situations in my life and how they shaped me as a human being, made me grow inside, and changed my values. In Barcelona, where I had enjoyed a comfortable lifestyle, I could never have imagined the sudden turnaround that my life would take. From having everything to absolute bankruptcy. But it was in those moments that I began to value the simple things in life, the selfless love, the feeling of home that was never instilled in me as a child. In my family, everything was "so much you have, so much you are worth," and, "the best friend is a dollar in the pocket." But in those moments when I had nothing, I discovered that I had much more than I thought. I was alone with my son in New York, yes, but my lifelong friends had shown me that they were there for me, because of who I was or who I represented. And my son loved me and needed me more than ever, which encouraged me to push on. It was the culmination of all those events that changed my mind, and I realized that of all the treasures I possessed, my son was the most valuable. A raw treasure, which had to be polished, but that would come with time and effort and the sacrifices I was willing to make. I just had to learn to combine my profession with the care and education of my son and find a way to be successful as a single mother and as a professional.

3. The third film that I recommend, completely autobiographical but really good, is *Freedom Writers*. It is based on a totally marginal high school in Los Angeles, where its students, immersed in an environment of drugs and violence, have no motivation to learn and get to college. However, the dedication of the main character in this story, an inexperienced teacher played by actress Hillary Swank, make an impact on these unmotivated teenagers, transforming their lives for the better. I saw this film after I was finally settled in Brooklyn, NY, and was able to get my own apartment. After finishing my contract at the Catholic school, I started working in private and semi-private schools in New York. One such school, where I worked for six months, was a semi-

private school for African-American and Native American students located in the suburbs of New York City in the Brooklyn area. It was a challenge for me to teach those kids, who looked at me as if I were from another planet. I remember that the schedule at that school was very absorbing. It started at seven in the morning and ended at seven in the evening. It was difficult for me to take care of my son while working twelve hours a day, so I found the ideal solution: I changed schools and took him to mine. The truth is, that stage of my life was so intense that I think I fell asleep even standing up. I was exhausted, I had to get used to the educational system in the United States, and the students lacked motivation, so I really identified with this film. *Freedom Writers* entertained me, and through it, I learned how to integrate into the new and diverse educational setting of New York City schools.

Of course, these films are only suggestions, but the stories they tell are based on real events and people who have outdone themselves. If they were an inspiration to me, they can also be an inspiration to you. While in my down moments, I watched these films and I thought, *If they can do it, I can do it.* So, I advise you to look for distractions that will help you grow and value what you have and what you will have. Every sacrifice you are making now as a single parent in pursuit of your dream will be rewarded in the future, rest assured.

4. The next movie I recommend, *Entre Nos,* is also based on a real story but is less known than the previous ones. I advise you to see it because it is really inspiring. In the movie, a Colombian single mother with two children is abandoned by her husband two weeks after moving to New York. The woman, who doesn't speak a word of English, has no job and no money and has to overcome many obstacles to survive. I also found it very interesting that the film stars and is directed by this woman's own daughter, Paola Mendoza. *Entre Nos* is a reflection of the harshness and grandiosity of life, the desperation and constant struggle to get ahead, and finally, the reward for the sacrifice and courage of a single mother.

To entertain you and encourage you to begin your journey to success, I recommend you watch videos or read books by coaches who have inspired millions of people and helped them improve. For example, I recommend Anthony Robbins and his book, *Unlimited Power.*

I want to emphasize that there are people who, in difficult times, take refuge in religion or yoga. I am in favor of doing so but in moderation. Some people practice it with such fanaticism that they lose contact with reality. First, you have to believe in yourself and have confidence in the fact that you will achieve your goal, and second, you must act with caution, always knowing that you are going with your child. Remember that your child should never be a hindrance but a blessing, even if sometimes your perception feels different. In the next chapter, you will know the reason I impart these words.

Chapter 3

BE CONFIDENT AND TAKE ACTION

Take Charge. When You're Clear About Your Goal, Strategize and Take Action. It is Time For Teamwork, When You and Your Child Must Work Together.

Believe in yourself and be confident that you will achieve your goal because you will, and then act, always bearing in mind that you are making this journey of life with an exceptional partner: your child. Sometimes the circumstances may be adverse. Life can take you in other directions, and you may feel paralyzed by a sense of failure, but remember: Everything is temporary. The one thing I have learned from experience is: In life, there is no such thing as failure. There is learning. We are all students and teachers at the same time. Our child can also become our teacher. No one has a handbook for raising a child, especially when you have to play mother and father at the same time. So, why not write that handbook hand in hand with your child?

On the one hand, if you pay attention to the external signs, you will see that the obstacles in your path—as you learn to overcome them—will make you wiser and will be of great help in this journey you have just begun. On the other hand, you may be tempted to leave your child or children behind and live with a relative, especially if you are starting out in another country. I will tell you that it is much easier to start the journey alone, but in the end, it is less rewarding. I know several Latin American parents who have come to the United States alone, leaving their family behind so that when things improve they can collect them. But that's a double-edged sword because, during that impasse of waiting, many things can happen that delay the reunion between parent and child. If you can, from the beginning, take the road with your child, you will go slower, but it will be a more enriching journey, and most importantly, if you plan your strategy well, you will reach the same goal and be happier in the end because you will have done it in the best possible company: your child's.

Right now, as I write this, my thoughts are on a friend I made during my stay in London. Her name is Julia. She is from Ecuador and arrived in the British capital at the age of twenty-two with a student visa. At age twenty-four, she made friends with a Colombian national who was British. Their friendship grew, and Julia unexpectantly got pregnant. When she confessed her pregnancy to him, her supposed friend completely ignored her and suggested that she have an abortion. Julia was clear that she wanted this child and decided to take on the maternity alone, becoming, after the child was born, a single mother. Despite the difficulties she found alone in a foreign country with a baby and with only a student visa, cleaning houses to make ends meet, she never thought of sending her child off to stay with a relative in order to have more freedom. On the contrary, she rented a two-bedroom apartment in a London suburb. She occupied one bedroom with her baby, and the other she rented out to another tenant so she could comfortably pay the rent each month. Four years later, she met her now-husband, and the family has grown. When I first met Julia, shortly after arriving in London, she told me her future plans with incredible accuracy. First, she wanted to become an American citizen, then she wanted to form a large family, live in a house, and, as if that were not enough, invest in real estate in her country. It's been ten years since we had that conversation. I still stay in contact with Julia, who is proof-positive that a single mother with infinite dreams can achieve them all, one by one. My friend is a clear example that walking alone with your child allows you to keep dreaming, and even if you have to walk slower, you can do so with more caution and strength. Julia was clear about what she wanted to achieve, and she acted and achieved it. Now, she's living in a house in the center of London and loving her large family. Bear in mind, she continues to work and live intensely while enjoying a well-deserved reward: the happiness of her family.

It is admirable how Julia managed to get by on her own as a single mother and never stopped dreaming. She only believed in herself and God. She is a woman of faith, and nothing and nobody could stop her. Beyond those accomplishments, she also inspired and served as a role model for her son. Proof of this lies in her son, who underwent her journey with her and is now an intelligent, studious young man with a promising future. Now, just think about it for a few moments: What would have become of Julia's life if she had given up her son to pursue her dream alone? She probably would have achieved them all but would have missed all the stages of her son's growth, and today, mother and son would not enjoy the close relationship they now have.

The gentlemen who are reading this chapter may think that it is easier to deal with situations like this if you are a woman, that men are more clumsy in assuming parenthood alone and combining it with their professional goals. Nothing could be further from the truth. I would answer that there is little difference between being a single mother or father, that the gender of the parent is irrelevant. What is really important is the love these parents feel for their child, along with the determination and commitment to go forward with their child until the end. I think there are single fathers who do a fantastic job with their kids, even better than the average single mother. I witnessed such a case firsthand when I was twenty-seven years old. I lived in Barcelona at the time, and through some mutual friends had the opportunity to meet an excellent person and single father at the same time. First, we were friends. Then, José and I were a couple for a year, so I was able to experience up close the life of a man who took on single parenthood. Jose was divorced and had full custody of his four- and nine-year-old daughters. Jose was a dentist and ran two dental clinics, so he was extremely busy. Because he was well off, he could afford to have someone take care of his little girls in his home twenty-four hours a day. I was much more immature than I am today and could not understand that man's absolute dedication to his daughters. Despite the help he had at home, if the girls got sick or needed him for anything, he would cancel everything else and prioritize them. His daughters always came first. My boyfriend was always available for his daughters, yet continued with his dreams of expanding his dental clinic and improving as a professional. When I became a mother, I understood that devotion and regretted not supporting him more in that critical stage of his life, when he had to take on the role of both father and mother, work hard, and on top of that, look out for me. I guess I had to keep flying, evolving, and pursuing my own dream until the end. That's how it was, and even though we separated a year later, I will always have Jose in my heart as a great example of a human being and father. Thanks to that very rewarding experience with Jose, I have decided to dedicate this book not only to single mothers but to fathers as well.

When I lived in England and my situation was precarious, I will say that there were several occasions when I could have gone my own way and left my son in the permanent care of other people. For example, after living one year in the hostel, I got our own place, and my mother, with whom I had resumed contact with, started to make regular trips from Spain to visit me. My son was almost four years old at that time, and his behavior was really terrible. I enrolled him in a school near our apartment. One day I got a call from the school because my son had almost broken a classmate's nose. Alexander constantly threw tantrums that lasted more than an hour, sometimes right in the middle of the street. Some of his meltdowns were so outrageous that on more than one occasion I the police arrived and interrogated me. My son was and is a real character. As one of his elementary school teachers put it, "Your son is a little boy with a great personality." One time he had me standing in the middle of the street in the pouring rain for over an hour while he bawled because I wouldn't buy him a bag of chips. On another occasion, while we were traveling in a London Underground train, my son grabbed the handle designed to stop the train in case of emergency, pulled it, and brought us to a screeching halt. I won't even go into the chaos that occurred as a result.

Plus, it was rush hour. Then the police came, all the riders got upset because they were late for work... Anyway, it was epic. I really had to exercise some patience—which has never my strong suit—with my son that day. In such moments, I learned to count to twenty instead of ten and to look for strategies to calm my son's constant tantrums. Imagine being alone in a foreign country with a son of such character, with few economic resources and poor English. At that time, I hired babysitters to look after my son while I worked. I'm not sure which sitter was the worst of the bunch. For example, through friends, I hired an Ecuadorian nanny—a Spanish national—named Isabel who had just arrived in the UK and did not speak a word of English. I provided her with a job in a hotel near my apartment, found her a place to sleep for free, and even gave her a mobile phone that I had paid for. In return, she only had to help me with my son for three or four hours a day. So, although I thought I was pretty good to Isabel, I had to throw her out after a week. I would come home from work late at night and Isabel and my son would be gone. One evening, ten o'clock came and went, and they still weren't home. They arrived around eleven o'clock, and when I asked Isabel where they had been, she confessed to me in all tranquility that she had taken my child to a party. I could not believe it.

Such experiences with nannies and babysitters made me suspicious. In the UK, both types of caretakers are officially registered, but the sitter works from home. Because of my distrust, it became difficult for me to have a social life, and when I could arrange to go out at night with friends I would always end up canceling, either because my son suddenly became ill or because the nanny stood me up at the last minute.

Not only did I have trouble finding a responsible caregiver for my son but the gray skies and rainy weather of London also had me permanently shut in. It was during this hard time in my life, because of my lack of freedom, that I learned what sacrifice was with a capital "S." I have never been a depressive person by nature, otherwise, I would not have survived this experience, during which I didn't feel like I could be myself. The positive thing about those seven years living in the British capital is that I grew by leaps and bounds, learned humility, and learned who my real friends were and how to value them.

My mother, during her visits to London to see me, noticed the uncontrolled behavior of my son, and at one point advised me to "send him for a while with some relative so I can breathe easy and start having a life." I won't deny that I thought about it, but I still chose not to do it.

I always kept my goal in mind: to live in the United States, return to journalism, continue teaching, continue to prosper, and of course, make my son happy and a helpful partner in my life. I didn't know exactly how I would achieve all of this; I just knew that I would. So, I decided my son and I would walk that long road from Spain and England to achieve my dream together, and that I would wait for Alexander in London—so that my kid could accompany me to the United States. I had to work and act with strength and determination in order to find the patience to deal with a small child and, at the same time, cope with the different situations I was facing.

So far, I've mentioned two examples of single mothers with little economic resources and one example of a great single father, Jose, who dealt with two children alone and came out on top. This is my advice to you: When you are clear about what you want, be strong and take action without letting your child be taken away from you. You may question what's best at times, especially if your child is as mischievous as mine was. Well, I finally found a way to channel my son's character in a productive direction and help him find his own future vocation. I'll tell you about that in the next chapter.

Chapter 4

GUIDE YOUR KID TO SUCCESS

Guide Your Children to Find Their Own Way While You Pursue Your Dream as a Single Parent. And Learn Strategies On How to Deal With Your Kids If They Are Rebellious or Defiant.

In the previous chapter, I described some of my experiences with my son as a single mother and how difficult it was for me to deal with his behavior. The truth is that my son was one enormous baby, and that made things quite difficult. At four months old, he looked like he was a year old. He weighed over 66 pounds by age three. At age six he began to throw huge tantrums. Some people who witnessed these meltdowns and my inability to handle them advised me to give him a good spanking, but I was never sure if that was the best solution. Perhaps it was because my brothers and I were beaten so badly by our father when we were children. I remember, when I was five years old, my father saw me take a dollar from the cash register to buy a piece of candy. He took me to my bedroom, grabbed me by the ankles, turned me upside down, and started swinging my body in the air, banging it against the wall over and over. If my mother hadn't come into the room at that time, I wouldn't be here now to tell this story. Back then, in Spain, parents beat their children, and nothing was really thought of it. Today, fortunately, in cases of physical abuse, there are serious consequences. I also remember when I was eight years old, my school teacher told my father that I talked and was very distracted in class. After that meeting, my father locked me in my bedroom for a whole day with the light off and no food. Despite how much time has passed, I still remember the cruelty of my father and his old-fashioned method of punishment. I held a grudge against him for many years. Today, seeing my father through the eyes of an adult,

I must admit that he was an enterprising man, immersed in his own personal frustrations that I would only later come to understand and that his way of showing love was to wrap us in material comforts. My youth was a time of material abundance but also of coldness and no family warmth, where the only important things were to work hard, accumulate money, and maintain appearances.

As I grew older, I was fortunate to develop some good friendships, to know other family circles closely, and to value all that money could not buy, such as family togetherness, a sense of friendship, love, loyalty, and compassion. Thanks to these experiences, my perspective on life changed, as did my way of thinking. That's why, when dealing with such a naughty son, I decided to put into practice what I had learned in other people's homes, to motivate instead of hitting, to give affection instead of creating resentment. I chose to look for more educational techniques to channel my son's strong character while always remaining a present, close mother and mixing in some extra ingredients: love, discipline, and few material things. That was the first strategy I used, completely experimental, and the results were amazing.

I want to emphasize that although I was born into a family of merchants, none of whom read a single book, I was passionate about reading. One of my great loves is to learn; that has always been a major facet of my personality. Later, I decided to transfer this passion for learning to my son, praying that all those activities in which I enrolled him at an early age would serve to improve his explosive behavior. To give you an idea of how dedicated I was to this plan, I enrolled Alexander at the age of four in ten different activities—such was my desire to channel my son's uncontrolled energy in a positive direction. I remember spending entire weekends driving my son from activity to activity, which took a lot of sacrifice and was incredibly stressful. I gave private Spanish lessons on Saturdays and had to choose between accompanying my son to his activities or earning extra money on the weekends. Of course, I chose my son. Even though I had little money at that time, Alexander was always my priority. If I earned less, I spent less, buying the basics, i.e., food and clothes, and little else. Luckily, many charities in London offered free or low-cost classes, and I took full advantage, signing my little boy up for dance, drama, karate, piano, violin, Mandarin, after-school activities, and his star sport, basketball. Since Alexander had a lot of energy, I thought that enrolling him in a sport would be beneficial. He tried soccer first but was a bit clumsy at it. Since he was very tall for his age, I thought he could try basketball, but in England, it was not a very popular sport, and the teams I looked into seemed hesitant to accept him due to his young age. I finally found a basketball coach, Sterling, who agreed to give him a test. The first time my son held a basketball in his hands and bounced it, I knew he had a special talent for this sport. He was accepted into the team, and so every Saturday, my son and I took the train to the sports center located an hour from our house and in the same building as the Peckham theater. Alexander trained with teenagers, as there was no team of kids his age. Practice would last three to four hours, and my son would end up exhausted. Sometimes he wouldn't want to go, but

I had noticed that, as a result of all that physical activity, his behavior had improved considerably, so I had to find a way to convince him to continue with basketball. He loved toy trucks, so I promised to buy him one truck a week if he continued with the basketball team. That promise worked, and every weekend my son Alexander went to practice and did all his activities without complaint. Thanks to all those activities, which I had chosen out of desperation, my son's self-confidence soared, and he began to develop qualities that in the future would prove very useful and open new doors for him. I've noticed that these efforts through the years have already begun to bear fruit. Because he learned to play instruments and got into sports at an early age, Alexander was recently accepted into a gifted middle school in Brooklyn, NY. In the entrance exam, my son had to demonstrate proficiency on the violin and in sports. Competition for a spot at this school was very fierce, but since he was well prepared, he managed to get in. It is worth mentioning that this school is one of the best in the city and has an excellent afterschool program—and it's all free for my son. I don't have to pay a penny. When my son's elementary school told me Alexander was one of the few chosen to enter, I was moved to tears. So many moments of persistence, of dedication, of almost giving up yet still moving forward came to my mind that I was overcome with an indescribable joy. And I, who am rarely prone to tears, cried for a long time.

So you see how all those activities, which Alexander continued throughout his childhood, shaped his character for the better and gave new meaning to his life. Alexander presently plays in two basketball teams in Brooklyn, practices at a competitive level, and remains passionate about the sport. My son still remembers those toy trucks I used to buy him week after week to motivate him to keep going to basketball practice. Of course, he is still a young man with a lot of personality, but he's learned to productively channel his energy and talents, all because in the past I chose to implement a completely different disciplinary strategy than the one I received. Because of this, I managed to give my little one a direction in life, an incentive by feeding his mind with diverse knowledge and his heart with music that has sweetened him, helping to make him a more thoughtful individual. As I write this, a Spanish psychiatrist I met in London comes to mind. She was a single mother and had three small children in her care: a boy and two girls. The father of her children was an American doctor who traveled every three months to England to visit them. Sometimes she and I would talk about the education of children, and she always insisted that children should not be forced to do something they do not want to do because that can cause them unnecessary trauma. For example, she enrolled her son in a drawing course. He decided he didn't like it, so she took him out of it the next day. I never agreed with that opinion, feeling instead that we should insist that our children participate in such activities, which opens up a wide range of possibilities and builds character. Besides, what they don't like today, they'll likely love tomorrow. The best proof is in my son and his rejection of basketball when he started. Now it's his favorite sport. He even told me that he wants to be a professional player. I advise you to sign up your children for various activities at a very young age. These activities will mold their character, give their life meaning, and when they grow up, they will thank you for it. Education is, without a doubt, the best gift you can offer your children, as it is the only thing that lasts forever.

Another decisive factor in inspiring your children is to give them hope—the hope that they can achieve whatever they set out to do in life. For example, one day we were sitting in our apartment in London, still deciding if we could move to New York. Alexander, who was seven at the time, said with a tone of disappointment, "Mommy, I would love to play basketball, but in England, I have no future because the sport is not popular here." My response was positive and hopeful: "Life goes round in circles. We're here today, and we're there tomorrow. If you want to do something, you have to think that you're going to make it happen, and you're going to fight to make it happen." In difficult moments, now that my life and determination have brought us to New York City, I remind my child of that conversation we had years ago and how you have to have faith, because the universe listens to our desires, and if we really want them, they will end up happening.

That's how I mastered "the shrew," as I sympathetically used to refer to my son, and helped him find his own way.

I know that the future is his and that in the end, he will have the last word in choosing his destiny, but I have given him the tools needed to make wise choices in life. I always tell Alexander to do what he really likes, but that whatever he does, he should do it well. I will say that I am happy to know that I have achieved my dream, and moreover, I have guided my son to seek his. Of course, other factors and people have influenced Alexander's temperament. For example, it's always wise to enlist the help of therapists and child psychologists to speak to your child if he's reluctant to talk to you, especially in his teens. I also think it is very important to provide a balanced environment for children where they can feel safe and comfortable. The need for parents, especially single ones with less time to spare, to carefully monitor the friendships their children bring home and how they interact with others on social networks, is fundamental. Obviously, as single parents, you also need to have a personal life. You shouldn't neglect your personal needs just because you are a responsible parent, but I don't think it's healthy for a child to see his or her parents bringing strangers home on a regular basis. I have always prioritized the physical and emotional safety of my child when inviting someone into my home—especially while living in a city as diverse and multicultural as New York. It is also essential to instill values of responsibility and respect in our children. Although sometimes it's a little complicated to be a mother and father at the same time, if you set rules and put limits on your children, everything ends up being easier. After all, habits and routines are important, and they improve behavior. I know parents who brag about being friends with their kids…and eventually, lose all authority over them. We need to encourage trust between parents and children, but I have made it clear to my son that at home there are rules to follow and that I am and will always be his mother before his friend. In my opinion, respect and clarity in the role that mother and father play at home are fundamental for the proper education of our offspring.

Returning to the central theme of this chapter, in my experience, I affirm that our children, however difficult they may be, can be guided to find their own way while you pursue your dream of being single parent. Both goals are compatible if you guide your child with love, discipline, and the right strategy. It is perfectly feasible, as you have seen from the examples I have given previously. Of course, another factor to discuss is how to allocate time to fulfill the career aspirations of both yourself and your child. In my case, Alexander was a basketball fan, so I spent almost every weekend on the courts. Unfortunately, for me, the only sport I ever found motivating is swimming. Yet I had no choice but to be there, supporting him. I say this with a certain air of resignation, but I'm still happy for Alexander, because basketball is his life, and I'm the one who instilled that passion in him. In the end, what is life without passion? Not much, really. On the other hand, Alexander has also had to sacrifice his time so that I could keep working and achieve my goal. In the past, I always combined my work as a teacher with that of a journalist. After winning my Green Card, coming to the United States, and settling into this country, which has offered me so many possibilities to prosper, became my dream, my passion. I knew that it would be difficult, but I would make it. I also wanted to dedicate myself to social journalism, work as a teacher in this country, and write a book in which I could share my many experiences, which would surely inspire other people to move forward. I wanted to do all that and more, but I didn't know when all these dreams would manifest. I just knew I had to keep fighting and not lose hope. Meanwhile, I went on my way in silence, with my son accompanying me to the recording studios and TV stations, waiting for me to finish my work. Then, two years after arriving in New York, I enrolled in Brooklyn College, where I spent three years earning my master's degree in education. Alexander was there too, always by my side, waiting for me to finish my classes—sometimes until nine or ten at night.

Obviously, my road has not been easy. It is hard to walk alone with your child as a single parent, but if you find a way to motivate your child, you can come to terms with and support each other, as I have shown in this chapter. Of course, you will have to listen to the negative comments made by some people who cannot understand you because they lack the courage to live their dreams. Of course, there are those overly conventional people who have nurtured the stereotype that children only grow up properly when there are a father and mother in the house. That is completely false. I have had to listen to such sentiments on many occasions: "And being alone with your child… Why don't you go back to Spain? At least your family is there. They can help you," or, "Why don't you send your child to your parents? That way it would be much easier to start, and you would have more freedom." Believe me, these people have never put themselves in your shoes. Besides, whoever believes that a child growing up in a single-parent family is destined to fail just doesn't read or watch TV…or probably isn't on social media. Many celebrities have been raised by a single parent, including

Bill Clinton, Al Pacino, Jack Nicholson, JK Rowling, Lance Armstrong, Eric Clapton, Barbara Streisand, Demi Moore, and Tom Cruise.

We all have dreams, but only the brave can find the road to success with their child and fight until they achieve it. A *brave* person, like you, who after reading this book will have more strength and clarity on how to act, especially if, like me, you are a single parent. Remember that there are no limits. The only person who can limit you is you. Break barriers, and dare to live your dream. We are the people who live on the other side. We have crossed the "forbidden" river, and we have succeeded. Here I am, waiting for your arrival. I hope to hear your story when you do.

Chapter 5

BE HUMBLE TO KEEP PROSPERING

Cultivate Humility and Give Up Your Lifestyle as You Move Toward Your Goal. Always Listen To Your Inner Self When Making Any Important Decisions.

It was the Greek philosopher, Socrates, who offered the famous phrase, "I know that I know nothing." These words have long accompanied me along my path, especially when have I slipped and fallen. I lost everything I had and had to start from scratch, with no money, no family, and no close friends. I imagine that many of you who are reading this chapter will identify with this situation, and if you are a single parent, you will understand how difficult it is to go through this kind of experience with a young child in your care. Remember: We're here to find solutions, not to complain or make excuses. Stay positive, and remember the words of Socrates, which inspired me to keep going when I was at a crossroads, not sure of which path to take.

In the previous chapters you learned that after you have a clear goal, you have to get going and act without leaving your child behind. During this journey, you will find many sweet and sour moments. When those sour ones hit, you must know how to handle them, and for that, you have to have a very good grasp of the word *humility*. To achieve your dream, you will have to leave behind people you love, material things, jobs, and perhaps even a comfortable lifestyle. Everything will likely feel left in the past during this time in your life as you concentrate on your new goal and move forward. Everything, that is, except your child. Remember that he must always walk with you. Keep in mind before you start this journey that the people who really love you will still be there at the end of it. I am telling you this from my own experience. Moreover, you will recover what you had a thousand-fold because, at the end of the road, when you can caress your dream with your hands, your degree of satisfaction will be such that you will feel completely fulfilled, knowing who your real friends are because without a doubt they will be there waiting for you.

Interestingly, a few years ago I read *The Alchemist*, a book by Brazilian writer Paulo Coelho in which the protagonist takes a journey alone to follow his dream, though he regretted having to give up his previous life to achieve it. However, at the end of the story, the protagonist understood that life was only a cyclical adventure and that in the end, all the questions and losses he had at the beginning of his journey were clarified and justified. This story follows the protagonist's personal evolution as he finally finds his treasure and meets his authentic self. It is a fictional novel but written with great depth. If you read it, you will understand better the message I am trying to convey. Of course, in this chapter,

I refer to real people, flesh and blood, like you, me, all of us who have dared to dream big and have decided to make our dream a reality.

I also want to highlight the importance of humility as an instrument to help us overcome the difficulties we may encounter during our journey—and I have experienced many throughout the years. I have had to reinvent myself because, as mentioned, I slipped and fell hard, with no crutch to support me. From then on, I started to slow down, because I was holding my son's hand and was his only protector. I knew that what would happen to me would also affect him, so I learned to be more cautious, more responsible. When I lived in England, there were many times when I isolated myself in a room, just thinking about what strategy to follow to overcome all the obstacles in front of me and reach my goal. One of my biggest stumbling blocks was just figuring out how to survive in a foreign country with a child so young I could barely work. In London, I started knocking on doors and signing up for very basic jobs that in Spain I would never have considered doing. In Spain, I studied Spanish philology at the University of Barcelona and obtained a Master's in communication sciences at the Autonomous University of Barcelona. Afterward, I worked as a teacher and journalist. But when I moved to England, my English wasn't good enough, I felt alone, and although I was hungry for new experiences, I was quite disoriented. So, I was humbled, I didn't mind starting over, and I accepted the first opportunity that came along. I worked for a few days in a fast-food restaurant, and Socrates' words often came to mind, because the simplest thing to do at the restaurant, like preparing a coffee, had to be explained to me over and over because I didn't have a good grasp of English at the time. I put fast food in the fridge for the customers who arrived at lunchtime and swept and did other tasks in which I was quite clumsy. Although I was paid very little per hour, I tried to do well, arrive on time each day, and get through the trial period so I could be officially hired there. A few days after I started, they notified me that they were happy with my work and wanted to give me a more stable contract. However, the irregular schedule they offered me wouldn't allow me to care for my baby, so I could not accept. But the experience was still profitable, and I got to exercise the same humility I now put into practice on all occasions, because I have discovered, with the passing of the years, that "I know that I don't know anything." When my English improved and I was certified as a teacher in the UK, I started working in schools through temporary employment agencies, but what they offered was so discouraging that I had to keep exercising humility and keep learning. I was sent to schools where I didn't even have the opportunity to teach. I would just be the teacher's assistant. I spent my days sharpening pencils, cleaning tables, and running the teacher's errands. On many occasions, I felt undervalued but knew I had to resist becoming discouraged and remember that this was just one more link toward the culmination of my dream. So I kept walking, obediently and without complaint.

And talking about exercising humility to achieve what we want, a friend of mine named Alberto, who lives in Barcelona, comes to mind. He wanted to work in an advertising agency. He hadn't studied advertising and had zero experience in the field, so he had it pretty tough. But he was adamant, really motivated, and willing to start at the bottom to achieve his purpose—and he set up a strategy to get results. He looked for the most prestigious advertising agencies in Barcelona, and when after a lot of research he had a clear idea of the agency he was most interested in, he started calling it almost daily, asking if they had a job as an apprentice for him. The answer was no, but he kept insisting and insisting, until finally his call was passed on to one of the managers of the company, who told him, "We don't need anyone at the moment. Send us your resume, and we will call you when there is a vacancy." But Alberto knew that this was not the best way to enter the company. My friend had next to nothing to write on his resume. Besides, he knew most resumes get tossed in a drawer, forgotten, and no one takes them into account. So, he took advantage of that unique opportunity to talk on the phone with that company manager and said, "Look, I'm really interested in working at your company. My dream is to be an advertising creative professional, and your company is the best in this field. I barely have any experience, but I'm willing to start by bringing the coffee if necessary. I know you are a very busy person, so how about I give you a call every two weeks to keep in touch?" Alberto's humility, persistence, and clarity of purpose moved that executive who, after a year of receiving calls, gave my friend his well-deserved opportunity. A few years have passed since then, and Alberto currently holds an executive position in that company, of which he is also a shareholder. This is a clear example of how humility, pursuing your goal with determination, and using the right strategy can lead you to success. Alberto was single and had no children, but in this case, that is irrelevant, since what led him to success was his self-confidence, perseverance, and humility. Those three skills need to be developed in us, as single parents, in order to move forward on our journey. The most important skill among these three, in my opinion, is humility.

Case in point: I had worked as a radio announcer in a popular radio station in Barcelona, where I met Roberto.

I was twenty-seven and had already enjoyed a long career collaborating with local radio and television stations when I was offered the opportunity to direct and present the daily three-hour program in Catalan, *Temps d' Actualitat*. My program was broadcast from nine to twelve every night and was heard all over Catalonia. On *Temps d'Actualitat*, I commented on interesting news, answered calls from listeners live, and interviewed callers who offered diverse and varied testimonies, some of which were really surprising. For example, on one occasion a young gypsy woman called and told me about the "handkerchief rite" that took place after her wedding, and how they could tell that the woman had arrived at her wedding as a virgin, thanks to this custom. The woman told me that after the ceremony, she and her husband consummated their marriage, and to prove that she was indeed a virgin, she had to pass the handkerchief test. That is, she had to show the family a handkerchief covered with her blood as a sign that she had finally been deflowered by her husband.

I want to emphasize that these were eight really exciting years of my life, during which I had the opportunity to meet many people, and where, through so many experiences shared on the microphone, I grew as a human being and as a professional in the media. However, I remember that when I started working at the station, not everything was easy. I was used to voice-over work, producing, creating content, and directing, but I didn't have the slightest idea of how sound worked or how to solve a technical problem. My and my colleague's show was live and without sound technicians, so the announcers had to do everything. At the station, they gave us some basic instructions on how the console worked, and then they threw us into the pool without a lifeguard. So, if you made a mistake or someone called you something insulting over the air, you had to figure out how to handle it yourself. It was a challenge that could leave you with a reputation for being down-to-earth and where the ability to improvise was the best tool we had. Unfortunately, left without any help from a sound technician, mistakes on our part were commonplace—and tended to be magnified when broadcasting live. This gave off a bad image of the radio station, and our boss would call us on the phone very indignantly, sometimes uttering offensive words. I was patient and listened to him without complaint since I was grateful for the opportunity he was giving me. I understood that I had to practice more since I did not introduce the commercials on time or accidentally pressed a button on occasion. But, returning to the subject of humility, my radio partner, Roberto, reacted quite differently. Roberto had a show that aired before mine, so when it was over, he would say goodbye and then introduce me to the audience. It should be said that Roberto was a very friendly and hardworking person, and at first, I did not understand when he told me that at most of his prior jobs he had been fired before six months. When I saw how he responded to the calls from our director, who was unhappy because Roberto did not know how to solve the technical problems of his program in time, I understood why my co-worker lasted so little time at those other companies. One day, when I arrived early at the voiceover studio and Roberto was still broadcasting, I heard the studio phone rang, and Roberto answered. I could hear the boss screaming through the other end of the phone and was stunned as I witnessed Roberto answer him sarcastically with: "Excuse me, sir. Who are you? Who am I talking to? I think you have the wrong phone number." My boss clearly didn't appreciate this, and I could hear his voice rising steadily in pitch through the phone. Then, to my amazement, Roberto hung up on him and continued to present his program without the slightest hesitation. I was left speechless by that reaction, which seemed devoid of any feeling and full of arrogance. That day I arrived home at about one in the morning, and as I drove home, I thought about what I had witnessed. I had trouble falling asleep that night. While it is true that no one, boss or not, has the right to offend or treat anyone so rudely, there are far better ways of dealing with situations like that. For example, I've spoken to my boss face-to-face, while always maintaining a polite tone and ensuring that my boss knew that I was aware of the fact that "who pays, commands." The truth is that Roberto disappeared from the station six months after starting, and with him, his program. Later I learned that his contract was not renewed, and I understood the reason why because I had seen his behavior first-hand. Roberto's lack of humility, or rather, his arrogance, caused him to lose a good opportunity, and I knew that this would continue to happen to him until he learned his lesson. I want to add that the conversation I had with my boss about my technical failures during the program was very useful. From then on, in the eight subsequent years that I worked at that radio station, whenever I made a mistake (and I made many) he would call me to discuss it, but he never raised his voice to me again. There are always productive ways to deal with adverse situations in the workplace—and using humility is undoubtedly one of the best strategies.

On many occasions, we have to leave behind our old, comfortable lifestyle to immerse ourselves in other realities and new challenges. Leaving behind our comfort zone is an uphill battle, especially when you are a single parent. Changing your life means losing a lot of your old privileges. However, even though it may not feel worth it right now, this incipient journey you have just undertaken deserves all the renunciations you have to make. When you find the lighthouse—the big sign that will guide you to your goal, you will begin to understand why you had to leave so much behind, and you'll know that you had to do it to move toward your dream. The lighthouse is just that bright signal that launches your new life and shows the way forward. Once we find our lighthouse, there's no more uncertainty. The path to follow becomes clear and unambiguous. That does not mean that our path is without thorns, but we will know that it is the right one. I found my lighthouse when I held my Green Card in my hands. I knew that this was my path and that nothing and no one was going to take me away from it, that I would go all the way despite the temptations I faced during the journey and all the opinions I had to listen to that were against my decision. Perhaps the most difficult thing was to leave the people I loved behind since material things come and go. However, I am of the firm conviction that the people who love you end up returning, waiting for you at the end of the road because *love* knows no physical or temporal boundaries. *It is always there*, despite the circumstances that surround us. But I will talk about that in another chapter.

Remember that this is the right attitude to move forward, to find "your lighthouse," your "life motivator," that is, your motivation in life, and let yourself be guided by it until you reach your dream, always using humility. You will have to start your life anew, and humility is the most effective tool in these cases, believe me. So, take your child by the hand, and although sometimes it's easy to reflect on or yearn for the easier days you left behind, don't look back. Always face forward as you move toward that bright future that awaits you at the end of the road.

Chapter 6

SURROUND YOURSELF WITH POSITIVE PEOPLE

Surround Yourself with Positive People Who Offer Constructive Opinions and Help You Grow. Avoid Toxic Influences Who Distract You and Try to Divert You From the Path You Have Set Out on to Achieve Success.

First, I want to differentiate between negative and constructive opinions. The former is usually issued by people who do not know you well, and their opinions reflect their fears rather than their concern about your departure or change of life. Constructive opinions tend to come from your friends and family, from those who really care about you and see drawbacks in the decision you have made and in the challenge you have taken on to achieve your goal, especially because you are accompanied by your child. In this second case, people give advice from the heart and with the best of intentions, but this does not imply that they are right. If I had listened to my family's "advice" throughout my life, today I would be a different person and would not have achieved the life I am living. In moments when I felt unsure whether to follow someone else's advice that would move me away from my path, I remembered the words of Chris Gardner in The Pursuit of Happyness, the movie I recommended in Chapter 2. Will Smith, who plays Chris Gardner, is with his son in the attic of a building, where there is a basketball court. The son tries to shoot the ball into the hoop several times but misses. Will Smith tells him not to keep trying because he's not going to make it. His son looks at him very seriously and then picks up the ball in anger. Then Will smiles at him and says, "Don't ever let someone tell you that you can't do something. Not even me. You got a dream, you gotta protect it. When people can't do something themselves, they're gonna tell you that you can't do it. You want something, go get it. Period." I loved that advice, and I think it goes a long way toward embodying the message of this chapter.

Throughout my childhood, my father struggled to run a family business, and my mother quietly obeyed him. What my father said was law. My two younger brothers bowed to the directives my father gave them in their lives. And there I was, the discordant note, the black sheep of a patriarchal family who believed that as a woman I should not have dreams of my own, only marry and take care of my husband and future children. However, I was always a hard nut to crack for my father. While my family spent day after day discussing small investments and how to generate more money, I, at age eleven, read all the time. I started writing poetry, which was published in local newspapers. My father watched me out of the corner of his eye, and I remember how he told my mother more than once that "something was not right," because money was not important to me. That was not true, but those purely materialistic values my family had in which "money was God" bored me to death. When I reached adolescence, the differences between my beliefs and my family's became even starker. My father wanted me to become a housewife, to learn how to cook, and to serve him whenever he, as our father and elder, ordered it. But I wanted to write. I was a good student and dreamed of going to college, traveling, and having new experiences. One day I got my father particularly mad, and as a result, we all ran out of lunch. Allow me to explain. I was fourteen years old and sitting at the table with my mother and one of my brothers. That day, my mother had prepared lentils and a salad. I remember that my father asked me in an imperative tone to get up from the table and bring him a glass of water, to which I replied, "You get up." After that, I only remember the palm of his hand pressing hard against my cheek and how he got up, took his plate of lentils and, with anger, smashed it to pieces on the table. After that incident, we met with my high school principal. My father told her that he was seriously considering taking me out of that school because I had been disobeying him a lot lately, and he needed me to work in the family business.

In conclusion, what bothered my father a lot, as a good male chauvinist, was that I, as a woman, had decided to study and prosper. If my brothers had done so, it would have seemed more reasonable to him, but for a woman, what was the point of studying? But my decision had already been made. I wanted to finish high school and go to college, and nothing and no one could change my mind. In the beginning, it was hard to stand firm in my conviction because my family was very insistent and tried to boycott my desire to prosper on more than one occasion. Now I know that they were not doing it in bad faith. They believed that their advice was the best for me, but they were wrong, as time has proven. When I enrolled at the Central University of Barcelona to work on my Spanish philology degree, my family screamed at the top of their lungs. "What is the point of getting that degree?" my father asked me one day with concern. "I like writing. I want to learn from other authors so that I can finally have my own style," I answered. I will never forget my father's expression of astonishment. A week later, he knocked on my bedroom door to tell me that he was going to expand the business and set up another store and he wanted me to run it. Of course, I ignored his proposal and kept studying. This is one example of a bad suggestion from a family member. If I had listened to him, I would have strayed from my goal.

Another situation in which I stood firm, despite the bombardment of contrary opinions I received, was when I made the decision to leave everything and live in England with my husband and son. I still remember my family calling me crazy—I was going to leave behind two good jobs, one as a director of a local television station and the other as a high school teacher in Barcelona, and throw myself into a country where I barely knew the language, without a stable job or place to live. Why did I choose London instead of some other city? I had a friend in that city who invited me to stay at her house for a few days, and so I moved in with my son, who was only two at the time. I was overwhelmed then by many events that were happening simultaneously in my life, and I needed a change. For me, London was an escape valve, a link to change and to another path. And despite the barrage of criticism from my family and friends, I didn't think twice about it. I sold my car, left all my material possessions behind, and embraced the most incredible adventure of my life, where through a myriad of experiences, I would be tested as a human being, change my inner scale of values, and make a true survivor of myself.

I remember hearing several opinions expressed by people close to me in that period of my life, during which I was making a change of country and life and facing an uncertain future. A close friend of mine told me that she thought it was a big deal, leaving with a baby and without a stable job. Another friend advised me to stay close to the family, that no matter how bad things were for me in Spain, it was better the devil you know than the one you don't. But as mentioned, my decision was very well-thought-out, had already been chosen, and was immovable. Besides, I have always been of the mentality that life is short, and it is better to try than to live with unfulfilled desires. Back in 2008, after the real estate bubble burst, Spain was plunged into a deep economic crisis, which very much affected my investments. Despite this, my family and friends—always quite conservative in their choices—tried to convince me in a thousand and one ways to stay and avoid the risks that came with leaving my home. Looking at the situation through their eyes, I could understand where their fears came from, but I had already consulted with my inner self, and it had answered. I had to leave everything behind and start again. And so, I did.

You may find yourself in a similar situation and hesitate because your environment does not support you and you have to act alone. Do not be afraid; when your goal is clear and you feel you have to achieve it, go for it. I am one of those people who think that in life you should never regret what you do—just what you don't. A friend has told me several times: "But if I risk and fail, I will not be able to overcome it." Why cling to this viewpoint? To begin with, to make positive changes in your life, you must think positive. Repeat these words when you feel doubts, especially when faced with questions/comments from others. "There is no such thing as failure. There *is* such a thing as learning." In fact, we learn more from bad experiences than good ones. I know this may sound cliché, but it's true. In fact, people who have succeeded in their field had to assimilate many failed attempts before achieving success, yet they still pressed on. They were clear about their goal, changed their strategy again and again as needed, and persisted until they succeeded, without caring what anyone else thought. Examples include scientist Albert Einstein, actor Charles Chaplin, writer Stephen King, Ford Motor Company founder Henry Ford, and TV's Oprah Winfrey. It was Henry Ford who uttered this inspiring phrase: "Failure is simply the opportunity to begin again, this time more intelligently."

In my particular case, referring to my own experiences, I will say that I have made countless mistakes. Perhaps because, in the past, I was impulsive, not very cautious, and quite reckless. But on the other hand, thanks to my mistakes, I gained experience and wisdom, matured, and finally found my lighthouse—and with it, my path. At this moment I can honestly say that I am where I want to be, and of course, I want to continue improving. I have finally found myself. I know who I am and what I want, and that is priceless. If I had stayed at home, without moving a finger for fear of making a mistake, listening to all advice of others, I know that today I would regret it. Because I was strong and decided to move on, I was able to succeed as a mother and as a human being.

I have never understood, despite coming from a very traditional family and being educated in Catholic schools, why when you have children, and even more so when you are a single parent, society seems to impose more sacrifice on you than on others. A senseless sacrifice where one must renounce his vocation, his dream, for the sake of his offspring. That is completely absurd. There are many people who end up reaching a certain age and are overwhelmed by frustration due to not having achieved their goal in life, all because they let themselves be influenced and invaded by fear. Do not be one of them. You can do it if you put your mind to it. It's all in your mind and your heart. Break your barriers as I did and ignore comments that come from people who have had a routine life—and who possibly have had few mishaps in their life, so they have not suffered, but neither have they lived. The worst fate for me would be to live a gray, unemotional, boring existence. Believe it or not, a large part of humanity "vegetates" instead of living. When I was eighteen, during a strange conversation about death, someone asked me how I would like to be remembered when I died. I smiled and answered, "I want you to write these words on my tombstone: 'And she lived. So young that I was and so clear that I had it.' The years have passed, and up to this present moment, I have remained faithful to my philosophy of life. Of course, when you are a single mother, you have to be more cautious and think about the consequences of your actions, because what happens to you affects your child as well. Yet, you must continue to live differently and never, under any pretext, give up being yourself.

I want to share with you another part of my life, during which I received a lot of opposition from my family and friends. This occurred in 2015 when I lived in London and was preparing to start a new life in the United States—specifically in New York. After seven years in the British capital, now divorced and alone with my son, I had achieved job stability by working as a teacher in several schools. I had a very well-located two-bedroom apartment by the River Thames, near Waterloo Station and close to the city. I had a small core of friends who helped me to cope with the rainy and dull London weather. Everything at that time in my life seemed tranquil, which on the one hand gave me a certain stability, but on the other, plunged me into solemn boredom. At that time, I stopped dreaming, I stopped the clock of my emotions, slipped into a routine, took care of my child, and learned to wait. While waiting those seven years to obtain a legal permit from the court to move to the United States with my son, I looked for ways to distract myself in that great city full of culture, free museums, theaters, concerts, emblematic buildings, and pubs full of executives toasting with their beers. I decided to set up an online radio station called Spanish-Link Radio, where I dealt with current affairs while listening to music. It was an enriching experience because I also had the opportunity to interview enterprising people like Per Wimmer, who was fighting at that time—and still is—to achieve his dream and who is a source of inspiration for many, including myself. Per Wimmer is a businessman of Danish origin and a founding astronaut of Virgin Galactic, together with Sir Richard Branson. Per is based in London, and I had the opportunity to meet him, purely by chance, during a conference at the Danish Chamber of Commerce, to which I had been invited by a friend. I was surprised by the enthusiasm of his words while he was presenting his space tourism project. The sparkle in his eyes as he spoke about space flight, the passion with which he expressed himself, and his docile and energetic gestures, all struck me. At that moment I felt like I identified with that man, and I said to myself, "This was me a few years ago." That was when I realized that this was in fact a sign of hope life had sent me to get back on track, from which nothing and nobody could make me deviate. However, even though I was quite clear about my path to success, I did not count on my family putting so many obstacles in my way before I left for the United States.

Since I already knew that my mother is somewhat afraid of change, I chose not to tell her anything until the date of the trip was near. My mother called me once a week, and it was in January 2015 when I told her that I had already bought the plane tickets to move to New York with my son. My mother, upon hearing of my intentions, went insane. From then on, she called me every day, begging me to tell her that it was a joke and that I was going to stay in England because to go on a journey alone with a child was really crazy. I remember her words: "In London, you have a home, a job, a good school for your child. What more do you want?" And she was partly right, but inside I knew that I had to leave, that I couldn't miss the opportunity that lay ahead. When I would not give in, my mother's calls became more frantic and upset. She realized she couldn't change my mind and tried to coerce me, saying that I was giving her such a hard time that she was going to get sick. But even so, she didn't make me give up my purpose. You might think that I was very insensitive to my mother's reaction, that I should have stayed in my comfort zone and not complicated my existence any further. But I didn't want to continue vegetating. I wanted to feel again, to remember that I was alive, and that can only be achieved when you can caress your dream with your hands and hold it close. Despite my mom's desperate attempts to deter me, my inner voice told me to grab that opportunity without hesitation, that there was a lighthouse out there that would finally lead me to my dream. Luckily, in the end, my mother gave up her efforts to change the course of my journey. How did I manage to dissuade her? I told her in a firm and forceful voice to stay out of it, that I was a big girl, and that my decision had been well-thought-out. And it worked—my mom accepted my choice. I advise you to be passionate and sure of your words in situations like this. It will make all the difference, believe me.

By the way, I'm still in contact with my mother, and every time she calls me, she repeats: "Lucky you, daughter!" Do you think it's just luck? Of course, it's not. Luck is something you have to look for, and there are many components involved. In this and previous chapters, you have seen that several factors influence success—one very important one being the detachment to the material, which we will talk about in the next chapter.

Chapter 7

BE READY TO LEAVE SOME PEOPLE
AND THINGS BEHIND

*Be Prepared to Temporarily Leave Behind People You Love
and Material Things Along the Way to Success. Remember
That You Are Taking with You Your Most Precious Treasure:
Your Child.*

It is well known that we live in a completely materialistic world, where the one who wears the best clothes and owns the best house and best car, along with all the other comforts that characterize our modern society, reigns supreme. It is also true that when, for one reason or another, we lose these privileges that socially extol us as a superior being, we feel discouraged, and we don't know which direction to take. For example, there are people who, after losing material things because of a financial crisis, such as the one we suffered in 2008, came up with extreme solutions, including suicide. If, in addition to all these factors, we add in the burden of being a single parent, the circumstances can worsen greatly, and dealing with them can become much more complicated. Why? Obviously, it's because we have a dependent in our care, and finances are important in any household. However, I would accuse our typical parenting style as being the main culprit in our poor handling of any loss of social and economic status. Next, I'm going to tell you about an experience I had as a teenager, which later helped me understand that "receiving everything for free from our parents," and, "giving everything to our children," is not a good way to educate our children to be successful. We must teach them to "earn what they want." As someone once said, "You have to give them the rod to fish, not the fish," otherwise, it is, "bread for today, hunger for tomorrow." In this way, we also teach them to deal with the wheel of life, which is sometimes generous and spins up, and we prosper—while other times it spins down, and we suffer. It is important to know that everything is temporary and material things come and go, so you can always start over. In many cases, we must learn to be detached and leave material possessions behind, giving us the opportunity to move forward with our goals and to recover those material goods—perhaps at a value that is doubled or even tripled—in the future. Because in this life, when a door closes, three more can open, and it is then that we finally realize what we've lost can be recovered to a much richer extent. You just have to start over and "learn how to fish again." That's all. So, if you're going through a critical time economically as you're reading this, don't make a big deal out of it. Remember that I lived through that situation too and I was able to recover. Don't worry. Just consider it is as part of our learning process in this world. Sometimes we are on top of the wheel of fortune and get to enjoy what we have, and other times we get stuck underneath it. It is then that we must be decisive, look for alternatives, and learn to survive and fight to find a new path that will undoubtedly be more successful than our previous one. The fact is, from bad experiences, one emerges stronger and learns a lot. More than anything, you learn to value simple things and the people who really love you. I speak from experience, so I know what I'm talking about! Lose your fear of leaving behind material things if you must do so because in the end life will more than compensate you. There are some people who are very attached to the material, which can take the form of a house, inherited property, a high-paying job, etc., and they do it only for comfort. But our destinies are twisted in the end. Oftentimes, such people must eventually surrender everything and face the frustration of giving up their dream because of the attachment they had for their possessions. For example, I recall a bank manager I met when I lived in Barcelona named Miguel. He was a very attractive man, married with two children, and successful in his field. I was a client of his, and sometimes we chatted in the bank. One day, Miguel confessed to me that he had separated from his wife and that he had a girlfriend much younger than him. However, he told me that he was not going to remarry nor buy a house, that he wanted an easy life without any kind of commitment. A few months later, Miguel told me that his new girlfriend wanted to have a child with him, and after he told her that he didn't want to complicate his life, she ended up going to a sperm bank and having a child by an unknown father. So, by now you should have an idea of the level of carelessness with which Miguel handled everything in his life. Since we were good friends at the time, I advised him to take life more responsibly, to get more involved, but Miguel always told me the same thing: "I don't want to complicate my life in the least." However, to show you how capricious fate is, in 2008, when the crisis hit Spain and the real estate bubble burst, Miguel, due to bad management, was one of the first managers to lose his job. Miguel lost his easy life, and with it, his material possessions, as he repeated the same mistakes over and over again. Miguel was forced to give up his high status, and since it was the only thing he cared about, he fell into a terrible depression that almost cost him his life. Was it worth it for Miguel to cling to the material and make it the center of his existence? I think the answer is obvious. In the end, what prevails and stays with us is our affection for others, our authentic feelings, and our experiences and the people who accompany them.

Consider this interesting experience I had in my adolescence. I was about seventeen when I had a serious discussion with the girlfriend of one of my brothers. The girl was clearly worried when she confessed to me one day that my brother had told her: "Life has no meaning for me. I am sixteen years old, and I have everything: a flat, a car, a motorbike. What more can I ask for?" I was struck by those words, and they really made me think. On many occasions, I heard my father say that he wanted his son to have everything he didn't have, which he did. My brother, whose character was much more docile than mine, decided to work in the family business, and my father had lavished him with attention since childhood. As for me, I had decided to study and take a different path entirely from the one stipulated by my father, which provoked his anger. Consequently, my father deprived me of many material whims. What he never realized was that he was doing me a great favor. Because of my father's actions, my character became strong and firm. I had to find a way to earn a living and learn the value of things from a very young age. I managed to earn some money from private lessons I gave at home for a summer when, not even knowing how to hold a broom, I went to work as a nanny and cleaning woman in the house of an Opus Dei family with five children. The youngest was just a baby, and the oldest was five years old. So there I was, in my early twenties, scrubbing and changing diapers among other things, all of which I did not feel were in any way beneath my dignity. I have beautiful memories of that month of intense work because, although I ended up exhausted, Mercedes, the mother of the large family, was a charming person. I was also able to experience up close what life was like in a family other than my own, to be imbued with their values. I realized that they were sometimes a little tight on money, but they placed a great value on family and togetherness. When Mercedes told me that she knew my work was worth more but they couldn't afford to give me a higher salary, I did not complain. I just told her not to worry. Today, I realize that in those moments, on some subconscious level, I had already begun to exchange the material things around me for more spiritual values, like feeling good and being happy.

Of course, you may find the idea of leaving material things behind and detaching from them to achieve success a little outrageous. After all, you have worked hard to get everything you have—you're not just going to throw it away. You may also think that there surely must be a way to keep everything while you struggle to achieve your goal, and that will be your child's legacy. You're partly right, and I'm not going to be so radical as to tell you to give up your material possessions, let alone ask your child to give them up in the future. What I mean is that sometimes—though not always—the path you will take will be completely incompatible with what you have accumulated materially up to that moment. Or, to put it another way, you may be forced to give up your comforts to achieve your dream. You have to be mentally prepared for such a circumstance so that it doesn't take you by surprise. For example, imagine that a unique opportunity has arisen when you least expect it, that you have your goal within reach, that you see clearly that you are going to achieve it, but you must give up the economic stability you enjoy at that time. What would you do? You would probably tell me that alone and with a child, you would choose security. I understand your answer, but it is not the right one—not if you want to achieve success. If you take the easy way out, that is, settle for what you have, you will later regret it and blame your frustration on your child. What would I do under such circumstances? Well, I would do what I did back then, and I can say in all honesty that it works because it worked for me. I took the hardest path, walking alone with my son, leaving behind my family, my friends, and my financial security while living in the UK.

In early 2015, when the immigration lawyer I had hired in Miami to process the re-entry permit contacted me and told me that if I did not move to the United States that year, I would lose my Green Card, it created a conflict of interest for me. On one hand, I had a two-room apartment in a privileged area of London for which I was paying very low rent and even considering buying it. My work situation had stabilized, and my son had been accepted into one of the best Catholic schools in the British capital. So, the words of the Miami lawyer hit me like a bucket of cold water. Life had just put me back at a crossroads, and I had to choose, whether I liked it or not. I had stability in London, but in New York, I would have to start from scratch again, and this time I would be completely alone with my son. On top of that, I would have to give up all the friends who had touched my heart during my stay in England. The decision was really hard; someone else in my position would have likely succumbed to fear and backed out. But I did what I always do before making an important decision: I consulted with my inner voice, and I let myself be guided by it. My intuition told me that I had to leave, that this was the only way to prosper. To grow and to achieve my dream, I had to take that step forward and move to the United States. And that's what I did.

As for my apartment in London, I thought it was a good idea to keep it, because the rent was really low, and I figured we could come back often and keep in touch with my friends. Also, I figured I could leave that apartment for my son in the future. However, shortly after arriving in New York, I received an email from the landlord telling me that someone had notified them that I now permanently resided in the United States and that unless I returned to London, I would lose my home. Once again, I was faced with a choice: either return to my old life, full of predictable things, or continue with the uncertain adventure I had just embarked on, alone with my son in the city of skyscrapers. I thought about it carefully, reminding myself that I was getting closer to my dream and that material things came and went. So, I continued to walk the most winding road, which offered me the least guarantees, but in the end, this was what led me to my goal, to success, to where I wanted to be.

I must say that the most painful part of undertaking this kind of journey is leaving behind the people you love. You always think that you are going to lose them, because logically life goes on, and in its course, other people enter your loved ones' world, which can cause them to forget you. I am referring to a loving relationship, a close friendship, etc. I am one of those who believe that in life, you can have everything, and that if someone loves you, contact can be maintained, and the relationship can ultimately be re-established. If that doesn't happen, it's because the relationship was fictitious, non-existent. Until very recently, in modern society, it was commonplace to expect a woman to give up her personal dreams for the sake of her family. In some cultures, this remains the standard. Fortunately, things have changed in the Western world, although there are always exceptions, and more and more women are daring to pursue their goals without giving up the people they love. I think that success and relationships are perfectly compatible with each other. Likewise, more and more men are taking on single parenthood and moving forward as parents and professionals. I think that credit should be given to both sexes because in modern times, roles have changed a lot, both for men and women—and that's a good thing! It means that, as a society, we are evolving.

A friend from Barcelona named Maria comes to mind, with whom I lost contact in 2008 after moving to England. At that time, I was feeling bad about myself and needed a change of scenery. I wanted to start again somewhere else. So, I left Barcelona without saying goodbye. I know I did things wrong, and I always thought that my friends would hold a grudge against me. But, once again, life taught me a lesson that only proves what I said earlier in this book: that the people who really love you are always there, no matter what. This path that I have undertaken alone with my son has shown me my true friends and has taught me that even if, at a certain moment, you must leave them behind, you will get them back. Although we don't need to recover what we've never actually lost, right?

During my stay in the British capital, I received an email from Maria. At that time, I felt more recovered from my internal wounds and was able to face my past again, a past I had run away from, and with which I did not want to reconcile for a long time. My friend was the only person capable of achieving the miracle I needed, of pulling the thread that linked me to what I had been and to who I was then. In those moments I was a lost person, in search of my new identity. I, who had always been confident, had in the last few years lost any interest in growing. I just wanted to survive. It was at that low point in my life that Maria appeared, and as if by magic, changed everything. My friend, without knowing it, gave me back my identity, and with the sporadic visits she made with her family to London and later to New York to visit me, she also helped me regain hope. Through her, I understood the value of friendship and how friends end up being a reflection of oneself. Real friends nestle in our hearts for life and always walk with us, despite the physical distance.

I have known Mary all my life. I was her English teacher when she was fourteen years old, and from that point, we built a friendship that has lasted for decades. Maria is an enterprising woman, strong and sensitive at the same time—a magic combination that makes her a great person, and as she has shown me in my most difficult moments, an excellent friend. I am not very good at expressing my feelings in public, but Maria is a person whom I love very much and will always have a privileged place in my heart, no matter how much life goes by. Yes, I did have to leave Maria behind to continue moving forward, to find my way when I thought I had lost it. But in the end, all the pieces of the puzzle fell into place, and I once again regained my motivation and the desire to fight, to prosper, and to move forward. My dream of settling down with my son in New York came true. Since then I have dedicated my life to what makes me happy: teaching, journalism, writing, and of course, my priority: the care of my son. And for the record, I still dream.

That is why I encourage you to detach yourself from material things, to know that life can surprise you when you least expect it and that all the sacrifices and renunciations you make while in search of your golden dream will be compensated for. The tips I have written about in this book worked for me, and that is why I feel compelled to share them with you. If they worked for me, they can work for you too. Remember that I am like you, a person of flesh and blood. If I could do it, so can you. We all can; we just have to really want it and go for it.

There are many people who get stuck for fear of losing everything, only to regret it later in life. If I had chosen the easy way out and stayed in Spain or London, I know that today I would be overcome with a deep sense of frustration. Why? Because my dream was here, in the United States, and today I know that for sure. So I pursued it and fought until I reached it. And here I am now, where I want to be, happy to have achieved it and to be able to enjoy it. In your case, your dream will be different. You may want to go into medicine, become an actress or a lawyer, start your own business, etc. We all have our dream in life, which we must pursue, without regret over what we may need to leave behind. As you have read in this chapter, after your goal is reached your real friends will still be there, and the material things will be returned to you a thousandfold because you have learned "to fish." You have become a survivor, a professional fisherman.

Chapter 8

KEEP STUDYING AND PREPARE
YOURSELF FOR SUCCESS

Keep Studying, Prepare for When the Time Finally Comes to Face Your Dream and What You've Always Wanted to Achieve in Life.

Now that you have learned to follow the dictations of your inner voice, and you are finally on track and know: some techniques to help you deal with your child as a single parent, how to ignore the opinions that do not fit your goals, and the importance of detachment from material possessions and of embracing humility to achieve success, it is time to feed your mind. By this I mean you must continue studying and preparing yourself because, whatever your goal, you can already see it in the distance if you have followed this guidebook step-by-step. You may be halfway or a little further along, and you may just need the final push to achieve it. However, when the time comes, it is important that you are ready, as the competition today is often voracious. If you shape up, keep studying, and have clear ideas, it is only a matter of time and persistence before you achieve your dream. For example, right now I'm thinking about how many immigrants have come to the United States, many of them undocumented, pursuing the American dream of prosperity, and despite all the obstacles in their path, they have worked hard so they could afford to study and finally achieve their goal: to reach a certain status and even legalize themselves in this very competitive country. One example is Mexican chef Alfonso Verdis, who as a journalist I had the opportunity to interview for the local television network, Bric TV, in Brooklyn, New York. I was enormously surprised by the personal and professional growth of this man, who had entered the United States at only fifteen years of age, risking his life by crossing the border illegally. Later, once in the United States, he began to study and work as a dishwasher and thus prospered until he achieved the excellent reputation he enjoys today as a chef. Although he is now the father of a large family, Alfonso is still studying and striving to improve. This is a clear example of a successful person, despite all the obstacles he had to overcome. I recommend that you watch this report I made on chef Alfonso Verdis to learn more about his career and life experiences. You can find it at: https://www.youtube.com/watch?v=bAu-XQhX4yY&t=163s.

Another example of a successful person who had a dream and achieved it is Luis, a Mexican businessman and father of two whom I recently interviewed for Bric Radio in New York. Luis tried to cross the border from Mexico to the United States more than thirty times before he finally managed to get in and establish himself as a successful entrepreneur. In our interview, Luis told me how many difficulties he had to overcome and how he was still working toward improvement and expanding his business. Luis, like Alfonso, had a dream. He saw it clearly, outlined several strategies on how best to undertake his journey toward his goal, and fought until he achieved it. Both were humble. They did not mind starting from the bottom because they knew where they wanted to go and that reaching their destination was just a matter of time. They have prospered, yet they keep learning.

Sadly, I do know people who have been fortunate enough to enter the United States through the front door, that is, with a green card or with citizenship, but who were not able to take advantage of it. And the fact of the matter is that despite all the facilities this country offers to immigrants to improve themselves, including numerous scholarships, many continue to hold the same rudimentary job as when they arrived, such as cleaning or supermarket work. It's not that I criticize the people who work in these fields, not at all. What I do criticize is how little these people use the resources they have at their disposal and how they remain anchored in the past and fear prospering. For example, I recently went to a supermarket to shop and spoke to the deli clerk, who told me he was an American citizen. I asked him why he didn't go to school so he could get a better job. His answer was to shrug his shoulders, raise his eyebrows, and respond with, "I'm very busy now. I don't have much time." Another day I went into a convenience store with my son to buy a coffee, and the cashier, who was in his thirties, told Alexander to study hard because otherwise, he would later regret it. I spoke briefly with the man—also an American citizen—who explained to us that when he was younger, he left school and was now very sorry about it. When I told him that he could still go back, he replied, "Now I am too old to go back to school. I missed the train." Of course, these two people are just using excuses, because there are those who hide behind any pretext to justify the unjustifiable. These two men had every opportunity made available to them, yet failed to take advantage because they didn't want to. Alfonso and Luis had all the doors closed because of their immigration status, yet they figured out how to get around the situation, mold themselves, and grow. The difference between these cases is that Alfonso and Luis want to move forward and continue to train to better themselves, while the supermarket and convenience store employees, though they are legal in the United States, chose to relax, take the easy way out, and leave education behind. So, they have stagnated.

As a single parent, you may be thinking that your situation is much more complex. If you already find it difficult to combine work and care for your child, when are you going to find the time to study? That's where this example comes in—to show you that there are ways to do it. It will take sacrifice, true, but it is possible.

As mentioned, when I arrived in New York in 2015, my first job was as a part-time Spanish teacher at Bishop Kearney, a Catholic school. Later, I was hired at a charter school in Brooklyn, where I worked from 7 a.m. to 7 p.m. I was exhausted, so I later accepted a teaching position at a private school in Staten Island, where the salary was low. After all these work experiences, I came to the conclusion that even though I had reached my destination, if I wanted to prosper in my profession, I would have to validate my Spanish studies in New York and go back to college. At that time, my son was ten and still in elementary school. I had already had him change schools three times, so he was stressed out—and so was I. Just imagine that situation, and on top of it all, I had set out to get a master's degree in education that would take me about three years to complete. Studying for my master's was an uphill battle for me, but I had done a lot of research and knew that it was the only way to get a job in education with a good salary, a schedule that would allow me to be there for my son, and a plentiful and well-paid vacation. So, I weighed my options and, as usual, consulted with my "inner self." My intuition answered, telling me that this was the best way, not the easiest way to be sure, but in the end, it would turn out to be the best. Again, I didn't feel it was in any way beneath my dignity to start from scratch, despite having already earned a master's degree in Spain. I applied the same principle that I have advised for you to achieve success, gain humility, and persevere. After an interview with Professor Ralph Di Bugnara, director of the program, in June 2017,

I enrolled at Brooklyn College to start my master's in the fall. How did I handle my son? Very simply. I took him with me to college. I must confess that I was lucky because many of the teachers, after asking their permission, let my son sit at the end of the classroom for the duration of the class. Although I was lucky in that respect, it was quite hard for my son to accompany me to college almost every day, then arrive home late, and the next day, get up at six in the morning to go to school. Finally, I managed to achieve my master's degree in two and a half years with outstanding grades. I remember that during that period of time, I slept an average of three hours a day, since I had to study, work, and take care of my son and the house. These were years of great sacrifice on my part, but my son was always by my side. He lived this experience closely, and through it, I know that he learned how to move forward to achieve his own dream in the future. I want to emphasize that there were many nights after attending college that I, exhausted, fell asleep on the couch, and the next day woke up to the discordant song of three alarm clocks, a good shower, and two cups of coffee.

Fortunately, I could take public transportation. If I had had to drive, I would have probably skipped all the traffic lights.

While working toward my master's, I shared an apartment with a twenty-year-old American girl named Ana. I emphasize her age here because even though she was young and a citizen, she didn't seem very focused on what she wanted to accomplish in life. When I met her, she was working at a fast-food stand and had just left college because she found it difficult to combine work and study. After a few months of living together, my roommate asked me how I could work, study, and take care of my son on my own. She confessed to me that she was unable to move forward on her own and was surprised by my achievements. That day we had a long conversation, during which I explained to her what I did to prosper—all of which you already know, thanks to this book. Soon after that meeting, Ana began to put my advice into practice. From that day on, Ana stopped complaining when things didn't work out the way she wanted and instead started looking for solutions. She devised a strategy in which she would look for a job that would allow her to resume her university studies—which, this time, she planned to take seriously, even if it meant sleeping a few hours a day and sacrificing her weekends. I was surprised by the determination and firmness I saw in her as I watched the radical transformation her life underwent. Within a month of our conversation, Ana had re-enrolled in college and found a more flexible job. I would get home and watch her spend hours and hours in front of her books. Today, Ana lives in a small property she bought in New York. She is continuing her college career, with excellent academic results, and has just been promoted to a new job—at only twenty-one years old. Although we are both very busy, we keep in touch. I am happy that Ana has finally found her way and, most importantly, learned how to achieve her goal and succeed in whatever she sets out to do.

For those of you who are curious about my college education, I will tell you that I recently graduated, though I didn't stop there. Once I finished my studies I had to pass three official exams to achieve my current job: the CSTs, EAS, and edTPA, some of which I had to repeat on more than one occasion. But I was determined to make it and go all the way without excuses, so I set my mind to it and did it. My son lived and watched up close as I moved, step-by-step, through this overflowing stage of my life. Because of the sacrifice he also had to make along the way, he will never forget everything that he learned. In truth, it was an apprenticeship for both me and him. That experience united us forever and taught us that the word "impossible" does not exist and that with perseverance and dedication, any objective can be achieved.

You may feel hesitant or be chronically postponing the start of education or training that could help you evolve and improve your skills in your field of work. If that's your mindset, you need to change it and move forward. It will always be difficult to find the right moment to combine work, childcare, and studies. So stop thinking and jump into the pool. Do it now. When I thought about enrolling for my master's program in the United States, it was a delicate time in my life. I still didn't have economic stability, but I thought to myself, *Either I do it now or never*, and I enrolled in the course. Today I am really happy I made that choice, because thanks to those higher studies, I now enjoy financial and emotional stability, which has had a very favorable impact on my son's development.

Another thing that I have always encouraged and continued to pay for even when my salary was small, are the cultural, sports, and musical activities in which I have enrolled my son since his earliest childhood. Sometimes I could barely make ends meet because rent is so expensive in New York, but my son never missed a private lesson. How did I do that? Putting food on the table was always a top priority for me, but beyond that, my personal needs were set aside so I could save and Alexander could continue with his classes. Since I left Barcelona for London in 2008, I have never asked my family for a single penny. It was simple. I managed on my own, and I managed with what I had. Despite the economic hardships, I found myself in at the beginning of this American adventure, my son never went hungry. I always kept him informed of the money we had left and that "when you can't, you can't." I remember one occasion when I had just ten dollars left in my account to make ends meet. My son and I had gone on an outing with my friend Clara and her son. We were walking in a park adjacent to the Natural History Museum in New York. I remember it was hot, and the two kids, mine and hers, started running to an ice cream stand and asking for a chocolate cone. I opened my purse and realized I only had a dollar in it. So, I went into the museum and found an ATM inside—and that's when I realized that my checking account contained only ten dollars. That was all I had left for the month, and there was still a week of it to go. It was painful, but I had to tell my son to stop asking because we couldn't afford it at the time. In all honesty, I did tell my friend that the ATM wouldn't accept my card. Now I think I could have been honest with Clara and told her the real situation, but at the time I thought she would not believe me. I wouldn't have believed it myself if

I were her, especially coming someone like me who worked in teaching. The truth is that private schools are renowned, but they pay their teachers very poorly. That was where I was in my life at the time. That happened long before I finished my master's, which would forever improve the course of my life and help me understand that the best way to prosper and achieve our goal lies in education. Material things come and go, but knowledge is the only lasting good, the possession that no one can take from us, that accompanies us for life. Remember that as you invest in your education, even if you feel insecure doing so. And, above all, give that great gift to your child. Children imitate; they are like sponges. If your child sees you learning new things and wanting to prosper, he will follow your path, and you will get to see your success reflected and enhanced in your offspring.

As I mentioned, due to the musical and athletic training my son has received since the age of four, he was accepted into one of the best gifted middle schools in New York. Today, although he still has a big personality, he is a talented young man who loves basketball and has excellent academic grades. My sacrifice has begun to pay off, and I am proud of his and my accomplishments. This is a prime example of how you can walk hand in hand with your child and achieve mutual success. You may think my case is exceptional, but you're wrong. I'm a flesh-and-blood person just like you. The only difference between you and me is that I made a decision, a commitment. I made a plan. I understood that obstacles can be overcome, and I fought until I achieved my purpose. How did I get there? If you've gotten this far into this book, you know how I did it. Do the same, and you will achieve your own success. Everything is within your reach. It's up to you.

Chapter 9

TRAVEL, OPEN YOUR MIND, EDUCATE YOUR CHILD IN LOVE AND TOLERANCE

Travel and Get to Know Other Cultures Whenever You Can. Open Your Mind and Get Rid of Prejudices. Educate Your Child in Love and Tolerance and Then Achieve Complete Success.

We all know people who have achieved professional success and enjoy a privileged social status but who nevertheless lack empathy and tolerance toward others. In my view, success is accompanied by the mind and heart vibrating in the same rhythm. Success is a long and wide road of learning, and when we finally achieve it, we have to show that we have evolved, that we are better human beings. This implies being more tolerant and respectful of the people around us. Traveling, getting to know other cultures, and interacting with people from other countries is fundamental to opening our minds and properly educating our child.

As you know, I have had the opportunity to live in three countries. First in my home country, Spain, then seven years in England, and now in the United States. Aside from those three countries, I always say that I have traveled halfway around the world, and I still plan to see the other half. For me, traveling is one of the most enriching experiences a human being can have. I have always been of that opinion, though the rest of my family is quite sedentary. For example, for my family, a dream holiday is to spend a fortnight in a beachfront apartment on the Costa Brava, in Spain, and little more, or to rest a few days in a Galician country house. Of course, they always want to go on holiday without leaving the country, because, for them, Spain is the best country in the world. In this respect, I would say that my country of origin has a fantastic gastronomy, spectacular beaches, and welcoming people who make tourists fall in love with it. Still, you have to travel to other places outside the country to appreciate different aspects in the world. For example, Spanish Mediterranean cuisine is varied and delicious, but in Argentina, they have a finger-lickin' barbecue that is no match for Spanish meat. In order to discover such little details, you have to spend a few days in Buenos Aires, as I did, and taste their excellent cuisine.

The truth is that I began to travel outside Spain when I was sixteen, following a bus trip with my high school friends from Barcelona to Austria. Although some decades have passed since that first trip abroad, I still have vivid memories of Vienna and Salzburg, a bucolic city bathed by the Salzach River. After that trip, a deep passion developed in me to get to know other countries, cultures, and religions. Although I liked to read and could get to know other places through books, for me it was not enough. I needed to see those places with my own eyes, to interact with the people there. I needed to interact with the world with my own skin. I remember one night when I was eighteen, I passed in front of my parents' room. They forgot to close the door and, coincidentally, I heard the conversation they were having. My father was saying to my mother, "We're going to lose her. Barcelona will be too small for her. You'll see. She will end up living in the United States." Today I think my father was a visionary (without knowing it) because he guessed the country where I would reside as an adult. For many years I thought about that furtive conversation between my parents and their obsessive fear of losing me. In my view, geographical distance is irrelevant when there is love. That's what airplanes are for, I say. I think that the greatest concern parents should have, with respect to their children, is whether they are happy or not. But over time I have gained empathy for and been able to understand my parents a little better, especially my father. My progenitor was an energetic, charismatic man and a businessman to the core. He had a gift for understanding the facets of business. Like King Midas, everything he touched turned to gold. He worked tirelessly, but he also had many dreams he could never fulfill. Like many human beings, my father was conditioned by family obligations, by what others said and by social conventions that he did not have the courage to challenge. My father would have loved to travel, to know other places, to live new experiences, and I know this because he confessed it to me on one occasion. He never dared to follow his dream, instead turning to setting up businesses, generating money, and making money his god. I want to emphasize that my father passed away young, at fifty-nine years of age, with many, many unfulfilled dreams. I remember one of the last conversations we had shortly before his death. We were in the hospital, waiting for the doctor, and I asked my father: "If you were born again, what would you do again that you haven't done?" His answer stunned me. "I would study," he replied. At the end of his life, the man who fought so hard with me to get me to quit school and go into the family business—in other words, to keep making money for the company—understood the value of my dream. My father was able to see my evolution after finishing college and starting to work. He had stressed that studying was a waste of time, then he saw how I got a good job and how I later started to travel around the world. My father had the money, but he killed his dreams, limited his life, and closed his mind and heart to the world. At that time, I was just starting my professional career, and although my mother kept repeating "save, Daughter, save," I ignored her. I was thirsty for experiences, for people, for knowledge. Perhaps because I saw in my own family that money can turn you into a slave unless you know how to give it its place. I decided to invest a large part of my income as a teacher and journalist into traveling.

In my early thirties, I said goodbye to my father, who left the earthly world in a cold hospital room. I told myself that I was going to do what he, out of fear and prejudice, did not do: *Live.* And so that's what I have done until now, though in a more moderate way when my son was born and I became a single mother. But those desires of living intensely have always marked my life. I have had unforgettable experiences in unusual places that I never could have imagined. I have talked with people of all cultures and social statuses, all experiences that cannot be paid for with money. Remember, money comes and goes, and if you "know how to fish," and educate yourself academically and culturally, you can live anywhere, overcome the worst financial crises, and always, always come out ahead. I tell you this from my own experience and from what I have learned on my many trips. Because culture is not only learned in books, it is also learned by traveling and meeting people.

You may be thinking it's crazy to think about spending money on travel when you have a child to support and other priorities right now. I'll tell you that traveling is wonderfully crazy, one of the best investments you can make for your child and yourself. Among many other benefits, by traveling you develop empathy for others and get a taste of the elixir of life. If you are thinking that this recreational and educational activity is going to be too expensive for you, think again. I have paid in advance for trips and come across some great bargains. Now, you may still be sure that traveling is a luxury you cannot afford. But you can. What can you do? For example, instead of buying a new TV, I suggest that you save a little money each month for your trips. Of course, I also suggest that you buy your train or plane tickets at least six months in advance and do the same with your hotel reservation. Someone once told me: "The person who returns from a trip is not the same person who has left." That's a very true statement. You and your child will return different people, renewed after each adventure that you undertake in the world. Another recommendation I want to give you— and you should take this even more to heart when you travel with your child—is to take a lot of time to carefully plan your trips and write them down in your diary, so that you will always have them in front of you as a goal. So, if you felt unsure whether you could ever travel when you started reading this chapter, now you know the transformative power of travel, and you know that you can do it as well.

Think about the story I told you about my father, a great man who left his dreams on a shelf and settled for making money while telling himself, *I would have liked to travel but I'm too busy, so I'll leave that for later.* That "later" never came, and I watched as he invested in the latest fashionable TV, luxury restaurants, and really expensive beach vacations. If you want to put his lifestyle in perspective as far as achieving dreams go, my father did achieve his professional dream. He started from scratch and earned a reputation as a businessman. So, in that area, he succeeded, but his success lacked something. He needed to grow as a human being, to evolve. My father chose to move in a limited environment, with prejudices that he never rid himself of because leaving our comfort zone is not easy. That lack of openness deprived him of his own personal satisfaction, of complete success. So, my advice is that if you have come far and are nearly at the top, if you're so close you can brush your dream with your fingertips, if you start to experience success, do it totally and absolutely. To do this, travel, know the world, be a better person, and become more receptive to what is going on around you—and be more empathetic and tolerant. All this is achieved by traveling, interacting with people from different cultures, and opening your mind and heart.

Next, I'm going to share with you some experiences during my travels that really made me see reality in a different way and helped me succeed in several situations in my life because I've learned to judge people less and understand the world around me more. I remember a trip to Egypt that I had decided to make at the last minute. At that time, I worked two jobs: journalism in a radio station in Barcelona and teaching in a public school. I had a month's holiday and no one to spend it with because all my friends were working. I decided that I would go on holiday alone, and I remember that I walked into the first travel agency I found while wandering around the Eixample in the Catalan capital. There, I paid for two trips. The first one was to Italy and the second was to Egypt. In Italy, I was impressed by Rome, which I found to be an extremely interesting and cultural city, a live museum. When I think of that beautiful country, what comes to my mind are some words spoken to me by a Jewish merchant who managed a clothing store in the capital. After a brief conversation, he gave me this advice: "In life, you can achieve anything. It depends on you being patient and knowing how to wait," and he added: "Whoever waits, eats the pear." Those words touched me because I have always been very impatient and wanted things immediately. On numerous occasions, when I was about to lose a job opportunity due to lack of patience, I remembered the words of that merchant: "He who waits, eats the pear," and I learned to count to ten before making a hasty decision. When I returned from my vacation in Italy, two days later, I packed up again and headed for the Egyptian capital, Cairo. Cairo seemed to me to be a chaotic city, where the traffic lights are just there for the sake of presence since neither the cars nor the passersby respect them. Crossing a busy street there is quite a physical and mental undertaking. Although the hotel I arrived at with my travel group was a luxury one, I thought it was intense foolishness to visit such an emblematic place while following the protocol of an ordinary tourist. So, I agreed with a fellow traveler to rent a taxi that would take us to authentic areas of the city, where being a tourist was irrelevant. I wanted to taste the essence of that city, to mingle with its people, to get to know all the faces of that frenetic and exciting place, not just those seen by other tourists. I remember that the taxi driver warned us of the risk we were taking by visiting areas that were not protected for tourists after I asked him in English to: "Take us to a real place, one that reflects how the less privileged people live." And he did. He took us to a cemetery where people lived in the mausoleums. The taxi driver asked us for a tip to give them in exchange for letting us in and seeing how they lived, with the recommendation to entertain us a lot. We did so, and it proved to be a very enriching experience that made me value many things and rethink how others live. In the Western world, coexistence in mausoleums would be unimaginable, no matter how much poverty was involved. But in that corner of Cairo, that community showed civility and had a harmonious relationship with the two things that unite all mortals: life and death.

Another of my favorite trips was the one I made to Peru. There, I spent twenty days traveling around the country by bus with some friends. At one point, we stopped in an indigenous village, and one man from our group approached a woman, dressed in dirty and typical clothes of the country, and gave her twenty dollars. The woman seemed absorbed by our fellow traveler, though it was obvious she had no grasp of what legal tender was. So she just stood there, holding the note in her hand, looking enraptured, gaze lost in the distance, as we walked back to the bus. That experience made me feel insignificant. We in the Western world move mostly for money, and that woman, who lived humbly, didn't seem to give it the slightest importance. I want to emphasize that on that trip, I was very impressed by Machu Picchu, the empire of the Incas. We arrived there by train from Cuzco, and I remember how I fell in love with the positive energy that emanated from that place, full of vegetation, ruined but still filled with majestic buildings that inspired within me a feeling of freedom. Then we returned to Cuzco, where I was overwhelmed with compassion for all the destitute children we found in every corner. Later, we had dinner in a restaurant downtown. Before we left, I asked the waiter to wrap up some take-out for me. Back on the street, a little boy came running up to me and took the food right out of my hands. Seeing all that extreme poverty made me feel terrible—and helpless knowing I couldn't really do anything about it. In our country, we throw our food away and waste constantly, while in Cuzco so many malnourished children exist, desperate and more than grateful to snatch up a tourist's leftovers. I lived through many hard experiences, along with some very pleasant ones, during that trip through Peru, but perhaps the most emotional event occurred while I was onboard a small boat, sailing on Lake Titicaca, and accompanied by a guide who told us that the houses on that lake were built on reeds and that a large community had settled there. During the tour around the lake, we stopped at one of the houses, and I became very emotional when the family there decided I should be the godmother of their little daughter and attend her baptism. Of the several people on board the boat, they chose me for this honor. The ceremony was very brief because we had to continue our journey but still very special. A part of my heart stayed there on the reeds on Lake Titicaca. Though I've lost touch with the family, I still think about the life and fate of that little girl.

Another country I visited and have fond memories of is Sweden. I was in the company of my Swedish boyfriend, Tomas, whom I dated for a year and with whom I traveled almost all over Europe. His home country captivated me, with its friendly people, strong and independent women, and tolerant culture. I remember that Tomas always told me that I didn't look Spanish and that I was like the women of his country: strong. I will never forget the days we shared in the north of Sweden, sledding in the snow, and our times in the cold, spent sleeping in a hotel built out of ice. We enjoyed watching an outdoor production of *Hamlet* while sitting in 8.6-degree weather. All incredible experiences that shaped my mind and made it more cosmopolitan.

Next was my trip to India, a country characterized by its color, smell, light, and contrasting levels of poverty and extreme wealth among the population. I was impressed by the spirituality of the men dressed in orange and the men painted white. I saw women with faces burned by acid walking through the streets. In Bombay (now Mumbai), I saw something I will never forget, which should give you an idea of how rich, yet incredibly chaotic, the country is. I noticed first how crowded one of its main streets was. In the city's center was a road full of cars and cows, all moving very slowly. Along the sidewalks were open-air food stalls that lacked any hygiene. Yet, I also saw vendors preparing lunch on a small table, where some monkeys were sitting and where the food would later be put on sale. I also noticed pigs circulating freely in the area. But by far the most impressive sight was a couple who had put a double bed on one of the sidewalks and were trying to sleep on it amidst the chaos. That scene was unique; I'll never forget it. Just as unforgettable about my trip to India was the visit I made to Benares. There I witnessed a human cremation ritual in the river Ganges and vividly remember when they threw their ashes into the sacred river. It was an incredibly unique experience. Reading or hearing about this ritual doesn't do it justice. Nothing compares to seeing this tradition with your own eyes.

I could write pages and pages describing my experiences in Cuba, Russia, Argentina, Uruguay, Greece, and the many other countries I visited. Thanks to all these experiences, I've come to understand that we all belong to one race: the human race. Thanks to all the people I have met on my travels, I have learned to be more tolerant and to understand that success does not mean achieving a certain social status or becoming a millionaire. Real success happens when our experiences transform us as human beings, when they make us better and help us achieve not only professional but also personal success.

After my son was born, I stopped traveling for a while. As he has grown older, we have visited several countries together. I always tell my son that wherever he lives, he should be proud of his origins and grateful for life. And to you, who have come with me on this journey and reached nearly the end of this book, I give the same advice. I also encourage you to plan ahead for your future travels. As you well know, I am not strictly referring to tourist trips, but to trips that open your mind, feed your spirit, make you grow as a human being, and give your life real meaning after the well-deserved success you are about to achieve.

Chapter 10

BE GENEROUS AND GRATEFUL

Develop Gratitude and Compassion. Be Generous and Grateful. Give Back to the Universe All Good Things—Especially the Very Special Gift You Have Received.

If you've made it to this chapter, that's a very good sign. It means that you are eager to embark on your adventure to success and that your commitment is only a matter of time. If you have followed my recommendations chapter by chapter, you have an ace in your hand that will help you overcome any obstacles in your path and achieve personal and professional success.

My last—and tenth—piece of advice is, as you move forward and take steps toward your objective, set short-term goals that, once overcome, will be very useful in keeping your momentum up as you move forward. And, very importantly, every time you achieve one of these goals, give yourself a treat. Celebrate with your child and with those closest to you. Be generous with yourself, with others, and with life. I wholly believe that the boomerang effect exists. By this, I mean that if you receive, you have to give, and if you give, you will receive. This is just enough to bring balance to our universe. That is why it is relevant—even essential, I would say—that you practice "gratitude." Give back to the universe all the good things it has given you, which are many. Every time we say "thank you" from the heart, that we share, that we help others without asking anything in return, when we are giving and grateful, that positive energy returns to our lives and gives us strength to go on. You can start by developing appreciation in your immediate environment. Practice it together with your child if you can. That way he will get used to doing it himself in the future. As mentioned, children are sponges and copy everything they see from adults. Model such behavior for your child with small actions and share with him the gratitude that is in your heart after achieving your life goal, your dream, the gift you have received from the universe. For example, whenever we sit at the table at mealtime, I remind my son to be thankful for the food we are about to eat. That way, he gets used to valuing the little things in life and feels gratitude for them. You may not be a religious person, and you may find it unnecessary to perform these kinds of home rituals. I'll tell you that gratitude and religion don't have to walk hand in hand. I don't consider myself a religious person, but I do feel a deep gratitude for all the good things that have happened to me, and I need to express that. Sometimes we human beings think we deserve everything, and in such cases, gratitude can be interpreted as a symptom of weakness. I believe the opposite. In my opinion, expressing gratitude, precisely *because* it is an expression of humility, makes us greater.

Here's a clear example of gratitude at work. Nieves, a friend of mine who lives in the Corts de Barcelona, visits the local hospital once a week on average to talk to the sick patients and encourage them when they are down. When I asked my friend why she did this, since she doesn't receive any remuneration in return, she replied that life had been generous to her, and she feels obliged to respond in the same way. She also experiences great satisfaction when she helps others. Another example of gratitude is that of my friend Julia, from London, whom I previously mentioned in Chapter 3. I had told you that for several years she had been a single mother and had come through because of her determination and constant battle to achieve her dream. Well, when I lived in London, Julia organized several charity parties to raise funds and help people close to her who needed the money. One of the parties I attended was to buy medication for a friend with terminal cancer. The truth of the matter is, everything she has done for others has been repaid in full by her good fortune in life. Although I've used acts of extreme generosity on the part of a few friends as examples, let me stress that you do not have to do great works of charity. It is enough to give the best of oneself and help as much as we can within our own boundaries. This alone is a sign of gratitude and gives back what life has given us so generously.

In this chapter of gratitude and mixed feelings, I will assume that after reaching the small goals you have set for yourself during your journey, you will finally achieve your dream, that is, your final objective. Once you achieve this, I advise you to do this activity in front of the mirror: Observe yourself for a few minutes and think about who you were and who you have become. Review through your face the most decisive moments of your past. Feel the satisfaction of having overcome all the obstacles in your path until transforming into what you now are: a fighter. Then, return to your present. Appreciate all that you have achieved, with your child always at your side, holding your hand. Look with love at the wrinkles that have been born on your face through that magical journey that has brought you here. Then, pinch your arm. Feel how you vibrate with the universe, and trust that from now on, you will truly begin to live. You and your dream are one, body and soul. From this point on, you are the captain of the ship. You steer your vessel. You decide the course to follow, and nothing and no one can make you deviate from the direction you have chosen. You have become a leader, capable of breaking molds and inspiring others to move forward and succeed as you have. Starting today, you will understand that the mind knows no limits and that the word "impossible" has long since been erased from your dictionary. Starting today, you will continue to grow in gratitude and compassion and continue growing in your life goal and in supporting other single and non-single parents to break the mold and dare to embark on their path to success.

After this journey through your inner world, which you have just viewed through your mirror, I would like to suggest another activity—this time with your child. Go find that diary you started writing at the beginning of your journey, open it, look for the pages where you talked about your dream, your desires to achieve that goal that seemed unattainable and that you finally achieved. Select a paragraph and read it aloud, knowing that your wish has been fulfilled and that your child is listening. Words are powerful. As you speak them, feel the adrenaline rush through your cells, your mind, your soul. Experience the power of the words you speak aloud because they are as real as life itself. Now, your child also knows you did it, that you fought against all odds to achieve this well-deserved success. And now, here you both are, savoring it together—and you are still motivating your child to find his or her own way. You have been brave, and life has blessed you with a child who will follow in your footsteps and fill you with satisfaction.

When I reached my dream, I did those two activities, and the truth is that they turned out to be very enriching and rewarding, especially the one that included my son. I remember that as I stood in front of the mirror for the first exercise, contemplating myself, countless scenes from my past came to my mind. I was eleven again, my sensitivity right on the surface, writing poetry behind the counter of the family business while the customers came and went. Surprisingly, I can still remember my first poem, which I've included below:

By a great tree,

at the edge of an olive grove,

I saw a little girl crying.

I asked her what was wrong,

she wouldn't answer me.

I left in dismay

and I never saw her again.

More the next day,

someone was hawking,

that the girl who was crying had killed herself.

I wanted to know the reason,

I went to where the case had occurred

and once there, they saw my eyes with great amazement,

that the tree had been carved.

When I approached,

I felt a sense of love,

and when I looked at him or it (the tree),

I saw in him the girl with great emotion.

I turned around and left

because I understood that the girl

had died for him or it (the tree)."

I also remembered the turbulent relationship I had had for many years with my father and how this same relationship inspired me to improve, to better myself. The magic words my father always said in moments of difficulty came then to my mind: "fight, fight, fight." I thought of the Russian roulette wheel that had been my life when I had started out with everything: luxury, travel, money. At that time, I was more frivolous in my choices. I lived fast and did not calculate the consequences of my actions. Still looking in the mirror, my mind continued to move forward in time, and images came to me of my time in England, when I had to start from minus-zero alone with my son, and life taught me humility. It was then that I was deprived of all the comforts I was used to, and it was from that point on that my personal transformation took place. In those moments of loneliness and material poverty, I realized my inner strength. I began to have other priorities, and my scale of values changed. That stage of crisis was the trigger for my transformation. From that moment on, another person began to emerge, more authentic, more real. A woman who, thanks to the obstacles she found on her journey, learned to contemplate life, to savor it without hurrying, and who, after having a clear objective, knew how to take the road to success—alone with her child—with firmness and fortitude. A woman and mother who, despite the harshness of her circumstances, chose to walk with her son without letting go of him for even a moment. My transformation was slow, but it did take place, and with that change, I became a survivor willing to journey to the end of the road to achieve my purpose. That purpose was my dream, and my dream was my personal and professional success. Many questions came to my mind as I scanned my naked face in front of the mirror. And that's when I realized that everything that had happened up to that point was just a vehicle, a means for me to get back to my authentic self.

My imagination continued to travel back, to a time when I lived in Barcelona. I was eighteen years old and my mother's friend took me to a place where she hoped I might reconcile with my father at a time when we didn't get along. I recalled an old lady sitting in front of me who had predicted my future. A woman whom I had mocked at the time, yet whom I remember today for her wisdom. My mind flashed through all the people who had come into my life, most of them there just to push me to continue my journey, and a few who were always "with me," but waiting for me to finish it so that we could meet again. Through these memories, I came to the conclusion that we are all products of our circumstances and our decisions, and what in the past might have seemed crazy to us, today has meaning and vice versa.

Finally, another image, more recent than the previous ones, invaded my mind and made me understand how the universe is wise and, at the end of our journey, all the renunciations we must make take on meaning. The universe closes the circle, and what we left behind during our journey returns to us a thousandfold. The following experience is a clear example that the risk I took to reach my dream was worth it. My mind moved to New York, when I, newly arrived in the city, was walking along Atlantic Avenue, near

Barclays Center in Brooklyn. I remember that many people were walking up and down the street when I caught a glimpse of a cameraman filming several scenes in the crowd. Then I noticed that his camera had a sticker with the BRIC logo on it. I was curious, so when I got home, I looked up information about the cameraman's actions on the internet. I saw that the footage was being taken for a radio and television company, BRIC Arts Media, in Brooklyn, and the first thing I thought about was contacting them so that my son could produce a *Star Wars* show, which he was already doing on YouTube. So, I wrote them an email, introducing myself as a journalist, and I sent them some *Star Wars* videos Alexander had recorded. Two days later, the head producer, Kuye, replied that, for the moment, they were not interested in my son's show but that I should send them my resume. I was perplexed because at that time I wasn't thinking about myself, just about helping my son with his television project. Well, I sent them my resume, and I was the one who ended up collaborating with them—and I still am. Destiny or chance? As I said before, it is the universe that conspires to close our circle of life after achieving our dream so that what we leave behind comes back many times over.

When I finished the mirror ritual, I went to get my diary and flipped through it, looking for the pages I was going to read aloud. I then called my son over to accompany me during the reading. Finally, I found some sentences that I had written before leaving Barcelona, listing clearly and concisely my most intimate desires, and the dream I then thought was unreachable. I have always believed in the power of words, especially those that are written. I know that what we write with our hearts ends up happening. So, if you want your dream to come alive and happen, write it down in your diary again and again. Then read it with conviction and believe it, because the miracle will happen.

In 2015, I came to the United States alone with my son, with only $2,000 in my pocket and a dream. I could have chosen the easier way—to settle down in London and vegetate all my life. However, I decided to take a chance and embark on a wonderful adventure that has brought me to where I am today. At present, I am still dedicated to teaching, and thanks to completing my master's degree, both my working conditions and salary have improved considerably. In addition, since 2017, I have been directing and presenting, in corroboration with producer Ed Parada, the television program *Que Tal & What's Up?* which is broadcast on cable television in the United States. I have also begun to make small forays into the business world. And now, totally unexpectedly, the opportunity has arisen to write this book that, I hope, will help all single and non-single parents, regardless of gender, to find their lighthouse and achieve personal and professional success.

What I want you to think is that if I, alone with a small child, was able to get ahead in a city as gigantic and competitive as New York, you too can achieve your dream, whatever it may be. You just have to be clear about it, propose it to yourself, and follow the ten tips in this book that have been so useful to me.

I would like to finish this last chapter, and with it, this book, with some magic words that I wrote in my diary when I started this trip. Words that at the time I selected to read aloud to my son. And now, I want to share them with you. These are some verses I once read on the front of a building and that ultimately marked the course of my life. It demonstrates the power of written words, which can do everything.

> "Walking around here,
> don't lose your memory
> that life is the way
> that leads you to eternal glory
> if you use it to the end."

Note From The Author

O n many occasions, my friend Eva Badia told me that I should write about my life because of the many experiences I have accumulated through my travels and my profession as a journalist, but I have always been little inclined to reveal intimacies. However, in life, you can't say, "never again." Because of various circumstances, among them Covid 19, the opportunity arose to write this book full of hope and fulfilled dreams. In *Successful Parent, Successful Child. 10 Things Every Single Parent Needs to Know*, I have undressed myself in order to help you start your own inner journey, a journey of life toward your golden dream. Because we all dream. We all have unfinished projects that we forget in our desk drawer for fear of leaving our comfort zone. That is why I wanted to show you, through my own testimony, that you will always have time to start your journey to success and that you can achieve whatever you set out to do if you really want to.

This book is dedicated, in a very special way **to my son Alexander** and, to all single parents and their offspring, no matter what gender they belong to. However, I would like to extend this dedication to all the dreamers who never gave up and to all those people who are still in search of that lighthouse that will make their dream a reality. Start walking because, on the other side of the river, there are many of us waiting for you.

THANK YOU FOR JOINING ME
ON THIS JOURNEY

Alexandra Brauni

www.ingramcontent.com/pod-product-compliance
Lightning Source LLC
Chambersburg PA
CBHW022115040426
42450CB00006B/705